If My Table Could Talk

Insights into remarkable lives

Michael Wynne-Parker

AuthorHouse™ UK Ltd.
500 Avebury Boulevard
Central Milton Keynes, MK9 2BE
www.authorhouse.co.uk
Phone: 08001974150

© 2011 Michael Wynne-Parker. All rights reserved.

No part of this book may be reproduced, stored in a retrieval system, or transmitted by any means without the written permission of the author.

First published by AuthorHouse 3/28/2011

ISBN: 978-1-4567-7584-1 (sc)
ISBN: 978-1-4567-7585-8 (e)
ISBN: 978-1-4567-7586-5 (dj)

Any people depicted in stock imagery provided by Thinkstock are models, and such images are being used for illustrative purposes only. Certain stock imagery © Thinkstock.

This book is printed on acid-free paper.

Because of the dynamic nature of the Internet, any web addresses or links contained in this book may have changed since publication and may no longer be valid. The views expressed in this work are solely those of the author and do not necessarily reflect the views of the publisher, and the publisher hereby disclaims any responsibility for them.

To Thomas Michael Ward

Acknowledgements

I am indebted to all who have directly or indirectly assisted with the production of this book – especially all those who appear within it whose lives have considerably enhanced my own life and in many cases continue to do so. Exceptional assistance has been provided by Jelena Sahharova who has diligently deciphered my handwriting (a painful task) to produce a perfect manuscript – much gratitude. Thanks also to Vasily Polomnik and Jelena for compiling the photographic section and to Nick Stalder, my long-suffering literary excecutive. Also to John Beveridge, who gave me the idea to write as I speak, not as I ought to speak (with apologies to Shakespeare), Frederick Bristol, Giles Chance, Simon Dyer, Simon Gurney, Ayman Jumean, Irina Emtseva, Paul Bura, Sarah Ward, and Fiona Wynne-Parker for their encouragement, advice, information, and inspiration.

Contents

List of Illustrations	xi
Introduction: Earliest Memories	xiii
The Table	xv
Buying the Table	xix
1. Jenkins	1
2. Derek Neville	2
3. George Trevelyan	9
4. Connie Winn	16
5. Anthony Grabbe	23
6. Anthony Gurney	32
7. Victor Bristol	39
8. John Glubb	46
9. Walter Walker	54
10. Ralph Hammond-Innes	60
11. Sergei Rodzianko	65
12. Said Hammami	70
13. Jonathan Guinness	74
Images	79
14. Katarina of Yugoslavia	99
15. Brian Rix	104
16. Harold Macmillan	110
17. Terence Amerasinghe	113
18. J.R. Jayewardene	118
19. Nissanka Wijeyeratne	127
20. Dai Llewelyn	130
21. Cecil Waidyaratne	134
22. Margaret Thatcher	137
23. Maryam Rajavi	143
24. Jim Davidson	150
25. Shafik Jumean	155
26. Summer Watson	162
27. Vera Protasova	166
Index of Names	171

List of Illustrations

1. Archimandrite Count Anthony Grabbe, Norwich, 1970.

2. Victor Hervey, 6th Marquess of Bristol, Savoy Hotel, 1973.

3. The author with General Sir John Glubb (Glubb Pasha), Norwich, 1973.

4. Ralph Hammond-Innes, Count Nikolai Tolstoy and the author, Bury St Edmunds, Suffolk, 1975.

5. Sergei Rodzianko jumping Rosalynd without reins, 1912.

6. Portrait of the author by Sergei Rodzianko, London, 1974.

7. Said Hammami at a reception in Norwich, 1975.

8. Lord Moyne (Jonathan Guinness) and the Hon Desmond Guinness, Kadriorg Palace, Estonia, 2007.

9. HRH Princess Katarina of Yugoslavia, Tallinn, 2005.

10. Lord Rix (Brian Rix), London, 1981.

11. The author with President J.R. Jayewardene, Major Anthony Gurney and Madam Jayewardene, Manor Farm, Northrepps, Norfolk, 1981.

12. An informal glimpse of President Jayewardene's private residence, Ward Place in Colombo. Also present are Mr Laksman Wijewardene, Dr Amerasinghe and the author, 1981.

13. President Premadasa of Sri Lanka with the author and Dr Nissanka Wijeyeratne, ESU Headquarters, Colombo, Sri Lanka, 1982

14. Sir Dai Llewellyn, 1993.

15. Margaret Thatcher signing her memoir *The Downing Street Years* for Saif Gaddafi, 2002.

16. Jim Davidson with Simon Gurney, HRH Princess Katarina and Jafar Ramini, Carlton Club, London, 1996.

17. General Shafik Jumean with Saif Gaddafi, London, 1999.

18. HRH Prince Muhammad of Jordan with General Shafik Jumean, Amman, Jordan, 1999.

19. HRH Prince Andrew (Duke of York) with Summer Watson, London, 2000.

20. Vera Protasova, London, 2002.

Introduction: Earliest Memories

Let me take you to those secret places – the ones long hidden in the dark recesses of the mind but which, with little effort, can be produced and shared.

Come, let me take you to a garden long ago where he, a few months old, is lying in his perambulator. It's snowing, and he stretches out his hand to catch a snowflake. A wondrous glittering crystal from the heavens, but like much else yet to be experienced, it quickly disappears in the heat of his tiny hand.

In those days there were real winters in England, deep snow and persistent frost, hard on the feet of country men who trudged long distances to work. Cars were few and far between.

Later, a growing boy, he ran from rock to rock, nimble as a young mountain goat, peering into nests. High up on a mossy bank he gazed into the blue cloudless sky, surrounded by bluebells, cowslips, and primroses, a heady scent, a gentle breeze, remote, alone. He learned to savour pleasure in loneliness.

But back to the baby in the perambulator. Where is his mother, father, nanny? He is alone. Peer into his face, gaze into his eyes. What can you see? What of his future?

The Table

Eating and drinking are essential for human survival.

In prehistoric times man the hunter returned to his primitive home, a cave or simple hut, bearing the results of his sport – fish, fowl or beast. Meals were eaten around the central fire. Food was basic – meat or fish, wild fruits, nuts, and eventually bread and cultivated vegetables. The poisonous sugar was not known until Roman times. Ale and wines accompanied meals 3,000–4,000 years BC. Warmth, food, and alcohol must have made life bearable in the uncomfortable and often unfavourable conditions that mankind has endured for the majority of recorded history. It is difficult to imagine what conversation accompanied the meal around those primitive fires.

No one knows when the dining table first appeared. Probably, it was very long ago, before the time of the Phoenicians. It was almost certainly raised a little above floor level, and the diners probably sat cross-legged upon the ground. In Egyptian, Greek, and Roman days, the table had become the norm. Around it, fine foods and exquisite wines were enjoyed. Conversation flourished in all sophisticated societies. Food, wine, and conversation were enjoyed over one to three hours!

Food was never meant to be eaten in haste. Fine wine was always meant to be lingered over. The art of conversation has always been the hallmark of civilization. This is a far cry from today's all too frequent habit of meals on trays before the television – perfectly acceptable when alone, but rarely in company.

The "high table" surrounded by chairs was already known in Roman times and was famous in Medieval Europe. At least one main meal was held each day, often accompanied by minstrels' music. Conversation was often political and philosophical, as well as witty and entertaining, amongst the small minority of educated people.

By the sixteenth century, dining became "fashionable", and enormous trouble was taken over the preparation and presentation of food.

Perhaps the nineteenth century was the heyday of the dining table. Throughout Europe, America, and India – wherever the British, Russian, Austro-Hungarian, German, and French empires had extended their influence – great and grand tables were surrounded by the learned and fashionable, the sparkling and witty, and eventually the commercial and political leaders of their day. We cannot read the great nineteenth-century authors Austen, Tolstoy, Proust, and Trollope without being aware of the significance of dining.

The dining table had become a status symbol. Hostess vied with hostess to provide only the best – the best in food and wine – and attendees! Tables became very long. Thirty dinners were not uncommon in the great houses of Victorian and Edwardian England. There, as in Russia and much of Europe, the Country House weekend – lasting from Friday afternoon until Monday afternoon – was made up of meal after meal.

Right up to and into my own lifetime the privileged English day proceeded thus.

9 am breakfast – at the dining table. This consisted of a hot and cold side board from which one helped oneself to haddock, kippers, bacon and eggs, kedgeree, toast and tea or coffee. No conversation was allowed at this meal as the morning papers were studied!

Next course luncheon at 1 pm – perhaps preceded by sherry or gin. Two to three courses were not unusual with wine and coffee.

At 5 pm came tea. No not just a cup of tea but a meal, served round the table, of cucumber and egg sandwiches followed by an assortment of cakes, scones loaded with cream and strawberry jam and teacakes.

At 7 pm drinks were offered – champagne, sherry, gin, whisky and by the 1960s a range of 'cocktails'. Dinner would proceed between 8 and 9 pm. All would have changed into 'evening' wear and the gentlemen escorted the ladies to their places at the Dining Room table. The host would preside at one end or in the middle of one side, with the most senior woman present to his right, and usually the most beautiful to his left! The hostess (his wife) would sit opposite him with the most senior man to her right. Thus, guests were carefully seated according to rank and presumed importance.

In medieval times, "lower ranks" were admitted to the dining table but were seated at one end, the furthest away from the master of the house. From this comes the saying "seated below the salt". Salt was a luxury in those days and not lightly shared.

By the seventeenth century, the "lower ranks" were firmly relegated to the kitchen, where right up to recent times the butler would preside over his table for lunch and high tea, exercising just as rigorous an order of precedence as was used upstairs.

Dinner would today be described as a banquet. A first course of hors d'oeuvre with white wine was followed by soup with sherry. Then would come a fish course, followed by game or meat with a fine claret. Next would be served a pudding (today called a sweet) accompanied by a sweet wine, or in Russia and Eastern Europe by Tokay. Finally, a savoury – for instance, devils on horseback. At each place setting there would be an individual menu card handwritten in French.

At this stage the hostess would lead the ladies from the table to refresh themselves, leaving the gentlemen to their port (passed leftwards round the table, the decanter never leaving its surface) and "political" conversation. This often meant risqué anecdotes and cigars!

Finally the gentlemen would (often reluctantly) leave the table to join the ladies for further drinks, conversation, and sometimes card games or charades.

Clearly the table played a major role in the daily life of the privileged and pampered.

In my own lifetime the daily routine changed, except in a very few great houses, gentlemen's clubs, and palaces. All meals became simpler (though in no way of lesser standard), and the grand dinner just described became the "dinner party" that would be held from time to time.

Sadly, breakfast, luncheon, and tea have largely disappeared from the dining room except perhaps at weekends. The dining table still, however, holds sway in many houses in the evening, and it comes into its own, once again, for the dinner party.

Buying the Table

In 1975 I moved into Saxlingham Lodge, Norfolk with Jennifer Lubbock, then my wife. We were newly married and had inherited some furniture, but we lacked a dining table.

The dining room was a perfectly proportioned Georgian room with long windows overlooking the front lawn. It required an appropriate table.

A Georgian mahogany table to seat ten to twelve people would have cost about £30,000. That was money we could not spare! After considerable investigation, I discovered a talented craftsman in nearby Suffolk who was capable of producing a perfect reproduction of a mahogany original for £5,000. The work was commissioned, and in the spring of 1976 the table was ready.

I remember well the day on which I collected the table. Having loaded it piece by piece into the back of the estate car, nobly assisted by my brother-in-law Dr Stuart Jennings, I carefully drove onto the main highway, only to be confronted by a huge lorry speeding towards us in our lane! Only by swerving precariously onto the grassy verge did we avoid instant death. The table was not broken!

I have been very fortunate to meet, and in many cases get to know, some fascinating individuals. Life has never been dull because of them, and this book is a tribute to the colour, interest, and often inspiration that they have brought into my life.

I am especially grateful for this, being well aware that for many, life is humdrum and tedious. Not so for me. I cannot remember a dull day.

It has been very difficult to know who to include in these memoirs and who not to include. Not all those included are famous or of great standing, but all of them are interesting. At least, they have interested me.

I: Jenkins

We had a gardener called Jenkins. I must have been about five. He talked with plants (long before Prince Charles) and introduced me to the complexities of nature.

The greenhouse was my favourite place. There was perpetual warmth. Under the bench were hot-water pipes fed from an outside boiler, which must have kept someone busy day and night. On the bench dahlia tubers sat on a bed of rich Irish peat and were constantly watered until bright green shoots appeared. Later these were cut off with a razor blade and placed in a sandy flowerpot until they miraculously produced their own roots and became living plants.

Under the bench were thrown endless geranium cuttings that also produced roots to become next season's decorative flowers to grace the dining table. What variety of colour the geranium produces. They range from pure white to blood-red, like those frequently seen adorning window boxes, set off against gleaming white Mediterranean cottages under an azure sky. And there are so many delicate pastel shades in between.

This close observation of nature, constantly reproducing itself, stirred in me an undying belief in creativity and God. I had caught a glimpse of heaven in that greenhouse, and gardeners and gardens have ever since inspired my admiration.[1]

One day, hiding behind a dry stone wall, I saw the ambulance come. Jenkins stumbled inside for his final journey. A whole world had ended.

---

[1] Part of my admiration for H.H. Patriarch Kiril comes from his love of gardens and his statement that if he had not become a monk he would have liked to be a gardener.

2: Derek Neville

It seems a long time ago – and so it is – since I peddled my bike across the narrow bridge and up the drive to Itteringham Mill. I had heard a poet lived there and that his name was Derek Neville, and I was convinced I must meet him.

It was Norfolk in 1965 – a summer's day with not a cloud in the sky, endless open spaces, woodland and lush green grass. It was the land of watercolour artists – Cotman and Crome – and the final home of Derek.

Was it just by chance that I met this remarkable man who was only once to sit at my table amidst the glittering crystal and silver, a strange contrast to the poverty he had known and rejoiced in?

"No," he explained to me, "it is not by chance it is destiny that has brought you here."

And this was the first time that I understood the truth that there is significance in events.

I have long been lucky to tread that pleasant path which wends its way between the lowest and the highest and to feel at ease with most of them. Few amongst my "highest" friends met Derek, and with most of them – my cigar-smoking associates of London clubland for instance – he would have felt ill at ease.

Tisha Bowes-Lyon[2] was different. She had tasted the bitter side of life despite being born into the grandest circles, and she immediately clicked with Derek.

"He is a real man with no hypocrisy," she said – and Tisha knew much about men. She had recently suffered an acrimonious divorce from Oliver Tetley (he of the tea bags) and had become disillusioned

---

2   Lady Patricia Maud Bowes-Lyon (1938–1995)

with life. Only Derek immediately understood her; he was a patient and instinctive listener and quickly dispelled her darkest thoughts.

Tisha and Derek had a great interest in common. Both were vegetarians. Tisha played with it. Derek was in earnest. Both believed passionately in animal rights and were a thousand light years away from my hunting, shooting, and fishing companions.

I remember one day driving along a country road and slowing down to let a cat cross over.

"The cat must be rescued," cried Tisha. The poor struggling creature was at once taken to the local RSPCA.[3] A few days later its owner turned up, only to be greeted by, "Don't you feel honoured that your cat was rescued by a cousin of the Queen!"

To Derek vegetarianism was part of his philosophy of life. He simply could not understand how I could go to Scotland, idolize the stag, and then kill it. No argument that this was the least cruel of deaths a wild creature could suffer would remotely convince him, and the idea that God had created animals for the use of man was an anathema. And this was a challenge. But what I learned from Derek was that civilized men can agree to disagree, respect each other, and above all learn from each other. Therein is progress.

Derek was trained as a teacher, and remained a teacher throughout his life. And what a life! During an early vacation he set off from London to walk to Land's End. All he had on him was a little card on which were written the words "Derek Neville, in Search of God".

Comments the poet, broadcaster, and writer Paul Bura, "His life on the road, nomadic existence, and experiences among the homeless and down-and-outs were to have a profound effect on him ... from wayfarer he became a way-shower through his writings and poetry."

There is some mystery about Derek's life before he arrived at Itteringham Mill in Norfolk in 1954 at the age of 43. He had found his life's companion and wife, Mary – his "soul mate", as he described her – and had begun to establish himself as a poet and writer of some distinction. He was establishing a following of "seekers after truth" who occupied much of his time with correspondence.

---

3   Royal Society for Protection of Cruelty to Animals

That day when I first set eyes on Itteringham Mill and first met its owner, he had lived there for eleven years and had created an atmosphere of harmony and creativity that made an immediate impact on one. There was *something* special there, and I wanted to get to the bottom of it or even be part of it.

Of course, the Mill itself is remarkable. It nestles in lush landscape on the meandering River Bure in idyllic surroundings "far from the madding crowd's ignoble strife.[4]" Clearly Derek had discovered the perfect place to think clearly, gain inspiration, and write the finest poetry and prose.

The Mill is steeped in history which, of course, lends to its atmosphere. There has been a mill at Itteringham since before the Domesday survey in the eleventh century. The present structure was built in 1788 and ceased operating as a mill about 1933 when it was converted into a residence. It was used during the Second World War as an officers' mess for staff based at RAF Matlaske. In 1974, shortly before leaving the Mill and their premature deaths, Derek and Mary were touched by the presentation to them of a signed and framed map of Norfolk by some of these officers who had returned for a reunion.

Having met the man in his natural habitat, I began to penetrate something of his mystery through his writings. To my surprise, he presented me with a copy of *The Ceaseless Beauty* written ten years before (1955). It is signed "In friendship, yours sincerely, Derek Neville, 1966".

Derek's whole philosophy of life is summed up in that one volume – though greatly expanded upon in his numerous other works. The essence of his philosophy is the essential goodness of life and that the aim of life is to identity with that goodness to the extent that eventually evil is completely obliterated. He had certainly found God.

Derek was a rare person, an original, a mystic, and I imagined that he was a sort of St Francis and St Seraphim all moulded into one and completely at ease with God, nature – and *himself*.

Over the next ten years I visited the Mill many times, sometimes alone to seek out and talk with Derek, sometimes with friends to

---

[4] From "Elegy in a Country Churchyard" by Thomas Gray.

introduce them to the invigorating atmosphere wherein even the hardest hearts were touched by that *something*.

But it was also fun to be there enjoying the lavish hospitality: let Paul Bura speak again.

> The little time I spent in Itteringham Mill with Derek and Mary was a time of tea, toast, talk, honey and scones. Peace hung on the trees like blossom and each corner of the Mill was just a poem away from inspiration.

Bura, no mean poet himself, was able to penetrate the mystery of Itteringham Mill and more importantly Derek. They say it takes a mystic to know another, which is probably why I only *sensed* the atmosphere of place and man but never really felt I understood it.

Two indications of Derek's real personality were revealed towards the end of his life. The first is from my own experience.

My wife Jennie and I received an invitation at unusually short notice to dine with him and his wife Mary. It was a perfect early summer's evening, and when we arrived we had a drink – at least Jennie and I did, for Derek was teetotal – and were shown into a most attractive private room where the table had been set for two. Derek announced that we could talk later and, somewhat to our surprise, left us! A waitress served us dinner, which was delicious although eaten mainly in silence, and it was only after the coffee, when we were invited into the *sanctum sanctorum* – the library – that I discovered what had been behind the invitation.

"You know," he said, "you're a young man, and I feel you have a challenging future. You will, I think, greatly contribute to a cause of international significance."

It was at this point that he mentioned that he had to give me a "message from Goethe" and wrote out on the back of an envelope the following:

> What you can do – or think you can – begin it!
> Boldness hath genius, power and magic in it.
> Only engage, and then the mind grows heated.

Begin! And soon your task shall be completed.

I put the envelope in my wallet, feeling more than a little overawed, and went home. Within a few days, both Derek and Mary had died from natural causes. I looked again at the back of the envelope. It now seemed like a challenge from beyond the grave.

The second and final indication comes from Paul Bura.

The letter flopped down on the mat. One from Derek, the other from Mary Woolmer[5] telling me that Derek was dead. At the same time I found a bird trapped in our kitchen, hurling itself at the window, bent on freedom no matter what the cost. I opened the window and watched as it grabbed freedom with both wings. A poem for Derek came thick and fast and the final draft was typed within half an hour.

I was determined to get to the funeral, and my mother and sister Josie also expressed the wish to go. The journey to Itteringham Mill began on a golden day in summer. I planned to pick up Josie in Canterbury, then straight on to the Blackwall Tunnel and off to Norfolk. Things just didn't work out. I left in plenty of time but there was some strange spanner-in-the-works. Firstly, I got stuck at some lights for fifteen minutes near Canterbury. Realizing the lights were faulty (which dawned on me nearly twenty minutes later) I ploughed on to pick up Josie. This done, we were off again. After leaving the Blackwall Tunnel I followed the signs to Norwich … but ended up going in the wrong direction. How signs could turn themselves round I've no idea, but this happened twice. When we were really sure we were on the right road, the red warning light went up on my oil gauge. Now I had filled up with petrol and oil before the journey. What now? I stopped at a garage and filled up with oil and set off again at a pace. Twenty miles on the red light went on again. I couldn't believe it. Again I filled up with oil. But now time was seriously running low. After more oil stops I

---

5 Derek's assistant at Itteringham

arrived in Norwich. Again signs pointed in the wrong direction. By now I was desperate. I had to ask someone for directions to Itteringham. I spotted a lady in her front garden and asked her whether she could help. With a broad smile and a "yes" she popped into her house to get a map.

Fifteen minutes later, just as I was about to drive off, she reappeared with a piece of paper with exact directions. We thanked her hurriedly and belted off at warp speed!

When we arrived, the service was all over. The church was filled with trapped birds waiting for release from the vicar or verger or whatever. We walked back out into the sunshine.

The grave-diggers were at work. I remember the sound of earth on wood. The many flowers told us that this was Derek's resting place. We paid our respects and left.

I wanted to take mother and Josie to the Mill for tea. I wanted to show them the beauty of the place, the peace of the place, the place where once lived a mystic that I knew who wrote poetry that tore my heart out. I needed to do this.

We arrived. The place was much the same, though in different hands now. The ducks and geese and swans were still there, the jumping fish were still there, and most of the magic was still there. No longer a place for Derek's books, mind you. We took our seat and ordered tea and cakes. I asked the waitress if there was a village garage which might be able to look at my car; there was no way we could get home otherwise. The oil light was on all the time! She told us that there was and pointed out the way.

We sat and drank tea and ate our cakes whilst I talked of Derek and Itteringham Mill. We were just three people. My real disappointment was that I had planned to read my poem for Derek at the service. I really wanted to do that. I leant back in my chair. Suddenly there was a distinct two taps on my shoulder! I turned round expecting to see a friend of Derek's that I might have met during my other visit. There was no one there! My mother and sister looked at me in surprise. There was nobody else anywhere near me. I "knew" immediately who it was. It was Derek. It was Derek letting me know that it is okay, letting me know that he was there that *he* was okay.

We arrived at the small garage and the mechanic agreed to look at my car. After a few minutes of scrambling around under the vehicle, he told me that the rocker-box was missing and that was why I was losing so much oil, my car was a VW Beetle, and parts for it are not something you just happen to have around. You have to order them and they take a couple of days to arrive! Then the mechanic told me that – coincidentally – he knew of two old VW engines in a back garden somewhere twenty miles away. And what is more he would get on his motorbike and go and get me the much needed rocker-box! What was going on here?

Suddenly everything was being reversed. Things were working out. Off went our trusty and oil-stained mechanic who returned in just over an hour. The rocker-box was fitted in ten minutes flat and filled with oil (again). The mechanic couldn't understand for the life of him how the rocker-box had come loose because the other one that he fitted went on as tight as a drum. He was truly puzzled. The amount he charged was minimal and we set off back home … without a hitch!

"There are more things in heaven and earth, Horatio, than are dreamt of in your philosophy." Thus wrote Shakespeare,[6] and this sentiment expresses perfectly the lesson of Derek's life.

In my book *Bridge Over Troubled Water* I speculated that my "message" from Derek related to my contribution to the expansion of the English Speaking Union in South Asia. Perhaps it was. Or maybe not …?

---

6   *Hamlet*, Act 1, scene 5

3: George Trevelyan

Sir George Lowthian Trevelyan, 4th Baronet

Sir George Trevelyan loomed large in my early years. From him I learned something of developing *balance* in life – balance of the physical, mental and spiritual – and an abhorrence of extremism in politics and fanaticism in religion. George seemed to me to tower above other mortals, and his presence was magnetic. He exuded enthusiasm.

It was at Attingham Park that I first met him. Attingham Park is a magnificent country house in Shropshire, now owned by the National Trust. The setting is near perfection – an extensive park landscaped by Humphry Repton, including ancient woodlands and a deer park, an old-fashioned walled garden, and an orchard. Through the park flows the River Tern, later to join the River Severn near the park boundary. It was the seat of the Barons Berwick until that title became extinct in 1953. The widow of the last baron however lived on in her own apartments.

Lady Berwick was more continental than English and spoke with a seductive slight Italian accent, having been born in Asolo and brought up in Venice. When I arrived at Attingham in 1966 to meet George for the first time, carrying a suitcase, I almost collided into Lady Berwick, who at once invited me into her sitting room.

"You have come to sit at the feet of one of the greatest teachers with a great eye for detail – and he won't like your tie." At once she cut off a strip of colourful curtain with a large pair of scissors and wrapped it round my neck. "Now you have a tie to be proud of!"

At this moment I was rescued by the towering presence of Sir George, who with utmost courtesy led me from the private apartments of Lady Berwick. She was tragically killed in a motor accident in 1972, about the time of my last visit to Attingham.

If My Table Could Talk

I had heard about George from several friends, each of whom urged me to meet him and suggested that the best way to do this was to attend one of his, by then, famous courses at Attingham. None of my friends said *why* I should meet him, but their enthusiasm convinced me that I should.

In 1947 George had been appointed principal of the Shropshire Adult College which, upon Lord Berwick's death, was based at Attingham. Following the Second World War, adult education became the vogue, and it had captured George's imagination. His vision was that adult education held the key to humanity equipping itself with the necessary qualities to enable people to change their relationships both personal and international, to change the environment, and to bring about a new era.

George began to see ever more clearly that people must change their thinking, which should then lead to an evolution in consciousness. He fully expected that the years around the turn of the century would be a time of crisis that would also become a time of challenge and opportunity.

He was clearly a prophet! His teaching has become particularly relevant in the present world situation. George saw tragedies as a wake-up-call – an opportunity to change ideas, attitudes, and behaviour and to realize that we are all part of one global community. By the time I arrived at Attingham, George was confident in his philosophy and brilliant in its exposition. He was indeed, as Lady Berwick had said a great teacher.

And this is what struck me first. Having wearyingly staggered through English literature classes at school, I now sat at the feet of the master of English prose and poetry. Never had I heard anything like it. Poetry that had previously been dead came alive, and Shakespeare became the ultimate reality. On the practical side George taught one how to read poetry aloud, to pause frequently and absorb the *thought* behind each word. Following his simple technique one began to enjoy memorizing the words of Shelley, Keats, Byron, Manley Hopkins, and above all Shakespeare. There had never been a Hamlet like George's.

"To speak what we feel not what we ought to speak" was a significant theme expounded upon by George. He had no time for written speeches, believing that the speaker should first absorb himself in a subject and then speak without notes, empathizing with the audience. Of course he was the greatest orator and communicator I had ever encountered, and I have met no greater since.

George had been brought up in the era of great weekend country house parties, but these were confined to the privileged few. At Attingham he developed every course into a perpetual country house party, and all were invited regardless of class, politics, or creed. His great quality as a host was a major attribute that made him such a success at Attingham. His background and disposition fitted him superbly as the hospitable master of the house, concerned with the comfort and amusement of his guests.

How had all this come about?

George was born into a talented and public-spirited aristocratic family with a penchant for radical thought and oratory. His father, Sir Charles Trevelyan, was a Labour MP who became Minister of Education under Ramsay Macdonald's Labour government, while his grandfather had been a member of Gladstone's Liberal cabinet. His uncle was the great historian and Master of Trinity College, Cambridge, G.M. Trevelyan, a friend and contemporary of Bertrand Russell, who was himself a radical and outspoken aristocrat and grandson of the Victorian Prime Minister Lord John Russell.

George's first enthusiasm as a teenager was for caves – exploring a form of inner space that was later to assume another dimension. At university (Trinity College, Cambridge) where he read the family subject of history, the enthusiasm was turned outwards and upwards to mountaineering, some of which at least took the form of illicitly climbing back into the college. He also fenced, literally and verbally, taking part in university debates.

After a spell in Germany after leaving Cambridge, where he became interested in architecture, Sir George returned to England as yet undecided on a career. A friend suggested that he might go in for crafts, an idea that immediately appealed to him, so it was not long before he had signed up in a Cotswold furniture workshop at Chalford. Here he spent two years "in the bliss of creative activity", before the workshops closed down in 1937. He made many pieces of furniture that he continued to use throughout his life.

It was at this point that he met Kurt Hahn, founder and headmaster of Gordonstoun School, where he was offered a job to teach history, literature, woodwork and practical work, and outdoor pursuits. This gave him the kind of wider contact he needed as well as a full and busy existence. In 1936 George first had the idea of using some great country houses as cultural centres for everyone. It was the seed of a vision that was to find its later fulfilment at Attingham. At Hahn's suggestion he went to Denmark to find out more about the Folk High Schools and first came cross the "Doctrine of the Living Word", whereby teachers were to speak from the heart without notes.

It was in 1942, when he was 36, that George experienced an event that changed the course of his life. He had become interested in organic gardening (well before it had become fashionable) and had sought out the leading proponent at the time, Derryk Duffy, at Heathcote House near Aberdeen. Duffy in turn introduced him to Dr Walter Johannes Stein who invited him to attend his lecture on Anthroposophy.

To quote George:

> That lecture was a revelation. The agnosticism of thirty-six years faded like morning mist. The spiritual world-view was clear to me in its glory and wonder. I have no doubt that this event in my life was planned and staged by higher destiny and that the timing was ripe for a leap in consciousness.[7]

George continued in teaching throughout the War. He was commissioned as captain in the Rifle Brigade but was posted to the so-called "GHQ Travelling Wings" for training of the Home Guard in warfare. Appropriately his field was northern Scotland, where he was appointed as adjutant to the Highland Home-Guard Division based on Inverness.

Let George take up the story:

> At the end of the war I went down with jaundice and spent six weeks in an army hospital on a diet of boiled white fish. I came out looking yellow and shrivelled, as if I had been in Belsen.

---

[7] *Exploration into God* by Sir George Trevelyan, 1991

When I recovered and reverted to normal diet, I remember visiting one of the biodynamic gardeners near Nairn and being allowed to sit under a tunnel of green raspberry bushes and pick these delectable fruits and eat them direct and sun-warmed. It was a taste of heaven.

Illnesses often mark karmic turning points in a life. Certainly this seems so with mine. Gordonstoun had kept open my place, and I recall walking the six miles from Elgin to take up school-mastering again. Halfway I found myself going slower and slower, as if some invisible elastic rope was holding me back, or as if some angel barred the way. I can still picture the sandy road with a leaning Scots pine. I came to a standstill. There was no conscious reasoning. I just stood and then quietly turned around and walked back to Elgin. I knew that if I once entered Gordonstoun, my post-war career would be that of schoolmaster. Now I turned and walked into adult education and an unknown future.

The decision taken, all the enthusiasm for the concept of the cultural centre in the country house came flooding back. I would get into the new movement for the short-term residential colleges. To gain experience I decided to sign on for two years more in the army and take a post of instructor in the No 1 Army College at Dalkeith, which was running two-week courses on every conceivable subject to help men and women from the services to get back into civilian life and qualification. I took a post in the arts department, teaching history and literature, with the hope that in due course I might become a tutor in one of the new colleges now coming to birth.[8]

And it was thus that George, responding to an advertisement for a principal, arrived at Attingham Park.

I attended several courses at Attingham in 1966. They have left a clear memory of days packed with interest – and one of George's

---

8   *Exploration into God* by Sir George Trevelyan, 1991

messages was that to take a keen interest in everything that comes one's way is the secret of gaining a long and fulfilling life.

The lectures and creative workshops covered all aspects of literature, art, music, and philosophy. Before attending the Attingham courses and meeting George I had not read Einstein,[9] Jung,[10] de Chardin,[11] or Florensky,[12] nor had I attended Glenn Clark's[13] Camp furthest out in America (which I did the following year) to meet the author of *The Man Who Tapped the Secrets of the Universe* and to learn that the potential for genius lies within us all. I had not heard the words "connectivity", "relativity", "organic", "green", and "alternative" (medicine), and the internet would be invented many years later.

After meeting George I delved into science, psychology, philosophy, and literature, as well as developing an appreciation of Wagner and Beethoven who were frequently played and interpreted by him. Of course, one could not become expert in all of this, but one caught the excitement of discovery and George's infectious enthusiasm.

Looking back at George's great qualities, they are easily summed up. He was primarily a pioneer, showing that education in its broadest sense never stops until the day we die. He was a catalyst for numerous groups, societies, and organizations – some on the lunatic fringe. He never joined them, but he helped them all to divest themselves of the inessential and focus on the central theme of the disciplined discovery of eternal truths and universal laws.

He was a natural diplomat, a good example of which was the way he won over a rather sceptical Shropshire County Council to go along with what were for those days rather unconventional educational courses. He

---

9   Albert Einstein (1879-1955) was a theoretical physicist, philosopher, and author who is widely regarded as one of the most influential and best known scientists and intellectuals of all time.
10 Carl Gustav Jung (1875-1961) was a Swiss psychiatrist, an influential thinker, and the founder of analytical psychology.
11 Pierre Teilhard de Chardin (1881-1955) was a French philosopher and Jesuit priest who trained as a palaeontologist and geologist and took part in the discovery of both Piltdown Man and Peking Man.
12 Pavel Alexandrovich Florensky (1882-1937) was a Russian Orthodox theologian, philosopher, mathematician, electrical engineer, inventor, and *Neomartyr* sometimes compared by his followers to Leonardo da Vinci.
13 Glenn Clark (1882-1956) was a professor of literature.

taught me that diplomacy is an essential ingredient of success in any new venture. Above all George was a remarkable communicator with an enthusiasm and zest for life that left a lasting impression on all who met him.

He once sat at my table in 1972. My other guests had not met him before, but I knew that he would easily blend with all as this was his nature. He rejoiced in difference of opinion and vigorous debate. That evening, however, a general silence overcame personal conversation as George took centre stage mesmerizing us all with his eloquent wit and deep insights conveyed with a light touch.

Late that night, before retiring, I asked him what he liked to do just to relax. "See a James Bond film," he replied. And this he did the very next day.

4: Connie Winn

Connie Winn seemed to me to inhabit a magical world conjured up by much champagne in an atmosphere stimulated by exotic conversation, surrounded by amazing watercolours.

Her large rectangular table, seating at least twenty, held centre place in a room bedecked from floor to ceiling by watercolour pictures – beautiful, dramatic, and above all colourful – all painted by Connie. What a backdrop to superb and everlasting luncheon parties!

All her parties were summer parties, and summer in those days was long, lasting from May to October. Connie had her own asparagus beds to provide the first course – asparagus with hollandaise sauce, washed down with ice cold Chablis (*premier cru* of course). Then either cold salmon brought down from Scotland by one of her Scottish landowning friends or young Welsh lamb served with her own garden vegetables, accompanied by a delicious Chateau Latour. No one worried then about diets, so next came sumptuous puddings with delightful Sauternes. But we always returned to champagne to while away the afternoon in a way that would have inspired Chekov! There was no port served at Connie's parties.

I never remember visiting Connie in winter. She was a summer person who absorbed the Suffolk light into a metamorphosis of colour. She was first and foremost a watercolour artist with the emphasis on colour.

Oh Connie, I wish you were with us now with all your flair and style. But you would not like this computer age, devoid of grace and time. Instant communication, via internet and mobile phone which you never knew, has destroyed much of the mystery – that aspect of the time we used to have to reflect upon, appreciate, and enjoy life!

I met Connie through a mutual friend, Hugh Aldous, of Saxmundham in Suffolk. Two more different people it is difficult to imagine. Hugh was quiet and reserved, Connie vibrant and eccentric.

One day Hugh suggested I might like to go with him to visit Connie, of whom I knew nothing at that time, to see her house and garden close to the ancient parish church in Aldeburgh. Clearly he had known her since childhood, but not closely, and in those days people took time to visit their neighbours.

Of course, I was spellbound by Connie in her environment of tranquillity and beauty close to the sea, an ancient church, and extensive, well-cared-for gardens that seemed to creep into her house, which was full of more flowers and stuffed with fine furniture and paintings. I determined at once that if I was not invited by Connie, then I would invite myself – and the sooner the better – for a longer visit without the inhibiting company of Hugh. I sensed I had much to learn from Connie.

I was not disappointed as she, as though by telepathy, pressed home an invitation to lunch the following week. That lunch, however, was not to be. No sooner had I returned home to Norfolk than I received a telephone call from Hugh. Connie had been rushed to the Norfolk and Norwich Hospital for an urgent operation.

I felt that though having met her only once, I knew Connie well enough to visit her in hospital, and I did so a few days later, having learned that she had recovered enough from her operation to receive visitors.

What a sight! Her room was full of flowers covering every table, chair, and even the bed upon which Connie lay. More remarkable still were her two companions – a small strange-looking woman and a parrot. The woman with a squeaky voice said, "Who are you?" whilst the parrot cried out, "Who goes there?"

Connie silenced her retinue, bid me to perch on the side of her bed, and began to tell me her story.

She had been brought up in Aldeburgh, where the Winn family had been long established. Her father, Arthur Winn, was the chief historian of the ancient borough, and the family was well known and also knew most people (at least the interesting ones) in the area. The family also spent part of the year in London based in Chelsea.

Connie always wanted to be an artist and began drawing and painting from an early age. When she was eighteen, she enrolled at Camberwell Art School, where she eventually met and trained under the watchful eye of Vivian Pitchforth.[14]

Born in Wakefield, Pitchforth had attended Leeds College of Art with Henry Moore, Barbara Hepworth, and Raymond Coxon between 1914 and 1915 and again, after military service during the First World War, between 1919 and 1920.

He won a scholarship to the Royal College of Art, where he studied under Sir William Rothenstein from 1921 to 1925. Shortly after leaving the RCA, one of his first teaching appointments was at Camberwell School of Art in 1926. He was a teacher of the highest quality and taught at several London art schools.

He exhibited widely, holding his first one-man show in 1928 at the London Artists Association, and became a member of the London Group the following year, after exhibiting with them for many years. He first exhibited at the Royal Academy in 1922 and was elected an associate in 1942, becoming a full member in 1953.

During the Second World War he was appointed an official war artist with the Admiralty and travelled extensively around Ceylon and Burma. In the immediate post-war years, he took up residence in Durban, South Africa, and whilst there was instrumental in sending students to Camberwell. He returned to England in 1947 and continued to teach until the end of the 1960s, spending the majority of time at Camberwell and St Martin's, where he was the principal life class teacher.

One day as she was walking to her class at Camberwell, Connie noticed a pathetic creature lying under a seat by the side of the road. It was a child in rags, a young girl, and a surge of pity overcame Connie, so much so that she took the girl firmly by the hand and, forgetting all about school, led her home for a hot bath and change of clothes.

No, her name was not Squeaky, though one might be forgiven for thinking so. It was Smeekie, and from then onwards nothing would separate her from Connie. She became her constant companion, friend,

---

14 Roland Vivian Pitchforth, RA, ARWS (1895–1982) was an English painter and an official British war artist during the Second World War.

and assistant. Call it what you will, she was to become an indispensible part of Connie's life.

Smeekie listened intently as Connie continued to expound on her colourful life to me, her very lucky new-found friend.

And there were more revelations to come. Ten years after Connie had discovered the poor and forlorn Smeekie, a telegram arrived at Aldeburgh post office and was quickly delivered to Connie. But it was not for Connie. For the first time in her life Smeekie, received a postal communication. It was from a London lawyer informing her of a large legacy she had inherited from her, until then, anonymous father!

I don't think Connie and Smeekie ever understood how Smeekie had come to be abandoned or how her father, perhaps overcome by guilt, finally left her the handsome legacy. Suffice it to say that now Smeekie found herself to be richer than Connie! Such is the strange justice that governs the world.

Smeekie was endowed with neither intelligence nor common sense, but she possessed a loyal and loving heart, and without any influence from her long-time benefactress, she insisted on devoting all her new found riches to Connie's advantage. The system was very simple. Every picture Connie painted, Smeekie bought. Thus it was that Connie's house was completely filled with her own creative work.

This strange story explained to me why as a very young but enthusiastic collector of art I had not previously heard of Connie, even though she lived in the neighbouring county. Her pictures never appeared in the market.

Perhaps here I should relate that I had started to collect English watercolours when I was eighteen. On a very small budget, I sought out work by little-known artists from the early nineteenth century until the present, and I was especially attracted by colour. I was now keener than ever to revisit Connie in Aldeburgh, and this I did just three weeks after her return home and full recovery.

Finally I was at one of Connie's memorable lunches! Not that one could remember too much after the three- to four-hour marathon! Remember, dear reader, that I was a tender boy of twenty-two, still unaccustomed to drinking the huge quantities of lovely wines that were produced bottle after bottle at Connie's feasts. However, during the first sober hour of the entertainment – for so it could aptly be described – I made every effort to look carefully at Connie's paintings, and the closer my scrutiny, the greater my appreciation of her genius.

Appropriately, the first fellow-guest I was introduced to was Vivian Pitchforth, who, as I discovered later, had evolved from teacher to close friend of Connie. He had an enormous influence on her and told me that he had decided at her first lesson not to teach her about colour as he believed it would be wrong to alter her *own sense* of colour. He was right, as all Connie's pictures are characterized by a broadly painted, vivid use of colour.

Over the next few years, I was privileged to attend several more of Connie's "entertainments", meeting guests as varied as the then Archbishop of Canterbury,[15] Peter Pears,[16] John Betjeman,[17] and Dorothy Thompson.

Dorothy Thompson, the least famous, was the most interesting. She was ninety-three, deaf and going blind, looking after an ailing sister, and yet was in the midst of writing a book about her father, a well-known local clergyman. She told me that without Connie's support and encouragement, the book would never have come about. The book was published shortly afterwards in 1969.[18]

I can't remember at which lunch it was that I walked away with one of Connie's paintings. I do remember arriving home and gazing at it, and it remains in my possession today. Entitled *Under my Window*, it depicts Connie's favourite cherry tree, which then flourished under her window in Chelsea.

How soon Connie noticed that the picture was missing I do not know, but a week later I received a letter which I opened with the nervousness of a guilty man.

---

15 Arthur Michael Ramsey, Baron Ramsey of Canterbury, PC (1904–1988) was the one-hundredth Archbishop of Canterbury.
16 Sir Peter Neville Luard Pears, CBE (1910–1986) was an English tenor and associate of the composer Benjamin Britten.
17 Sir John Betjeman, CBE (1906–1984) was an English poet, writer, and broadcaster who described himself in *Who's Who* as a 'poet and hack'.
18 *Sophia's Son* by Dorothy Thompson

Dear Michael,

I said nothing as I saw you rise from the table, walk over to the wall and remove the picture. None of the other guests noticed, engrossed in alcoholic conversation. At first I was very angry – then I realized that perhaps I was the selfish one, not allowing anyone except Smeekie to own my paintings. So please keep it – and accept it as a token of a new friendship, but treasure it always – never sell it or give it away.

Yours ever,

Connie

What a relief! I was not proud of what I had done, and I only wished to buy the picture in the normal way. And now it was legitimately mine.

Connie sent me another gift – a limited edition of a catalogue of the works of Georges Rouault inscribed:

Michael, don't lose this book or give it away and for Heaven's sake read it and try to understand it.

Connie

P.S. I can't replace this something book.

Of course, I not only read it, I devoured it, and it remains in my library. I discovered in it part of Connie's motivation. Rouault was a lonely figure in modern art, standing in enigmatic grandeur in the vast panorama of movements, schools, and excursions that constitute the art of our agitated times. Good and evil, suffering and expiation, hypocrisy, resignation, faith, justice, and the "human condition" were his themes – and he was a magnificent colourist. Connie was not just taught by Pitchforth, she was inspired by Rouault.

Like my friend Tisha,[19] whom I had introduced to Connie and with whom she was a "soul mate", Connie was an almost fanatical lover of animals. Yet unlike many of that ilk, she first loved people and would reach out to help all she encountered, as she had done so many years before when stumbling across Smeekie. Thus, she was rewarded increasingly, until the very end of her life, with real and devoted friendships.

---

19 Lady Patricia Maud Bowes-Lyon (1932–1997)

5: Anthony Grabbe

Archimandrite Count Anthony Grabbe, later Bishop Anthony

He was my first Russian Orthodox priest, my confessor and my friend.

I was ready for his influence when I met him in New York in 1966. Baptized an Anglican, influenced by my Roman Catholic maternal grandfather I was encouraged in Protestantism by my mother, who despised – even hated – her father's faith.

This left me rather confused in my earliest years. I seriously embraced Protestantism whilst having a secret love affair with Romanism. But the former increasingly left me feeling that it only just scraped the surface of truth, whilst the latter appeared too authoritarian and pedantic.

From those early years, I had come to know Russian people whom we knew as "White Russians". They or their parents had fled the murderous "red" regime following the bloody revolution of 1918. They were the warmest and most talented people, readily embracing their adopted homeland whilst clinging to their old traditions, most of all their Orthodox faith.

In Norfolk our close neighbours were the Meade family. John Meade, of ancient lineage, often invited me to shoot (or attempt to shoot) his high-flying and challenging pheasants. After the fourth drive, luncheon was produced and presided over by Valentine,[20] his Russian wife. We sat on straw bales in a convenient barn protected from the Norfolk east winds (straight from Siberia) which, explained Valentine, reminded her of her mother's recollections of similar shooting days in old Imperial Russia.

---

20 Princess Valentine Galitzine

Valentine is a good example of those Russians who relish their adopted homeland whilst never forgetting their ancient faith. She told me of her frequent visits to London to attend the Russian Orthodox cathedral, then based at the aptly named Emperor's Gate.

It wasn't long before I also visited that cathedral where Valentine introduced me to Count Kleinmichel, the then treasurer of the church. Count and Countess Kleinmichel were extremely kind to me, inviting me to lunch after the liturgy. Upon hearing of my forthcoming first visit to America, they urged me to make contact with their close friend Andres Mendoza.

Thus in 1966 I arrived in America full of excitement and anticipation. My original idea had been to locate some distant Wynne relations who were last heard of in New York. After a few days trying to trace them, I gave up and instead telephoned Andres Mendoza who invited me to lunch at the Metropolitan Club. He had a special guest, he said, who he would like me to meet. That guest was the then Archimandrite, Anthony Grabbe.

Anthony made an immediate impact both in appearance and personality. He was already a "prince of the church", dignified, confident, commanding, and yet warm, approachable, and reassuring, with perceptive eyes that saw beyond the superficial. He was dressed immaculately in his black monastic robes, starched cuffs, and highly polished shoes – elegance personified. I was intent to get to know him.

Few lives illustrate more fully the tortured fate of the Russian Orthodox in exile since the Bolsheviks seized power in 1917 than that of Anthony Grabbe. Born in exile and forced to migrate ever westwards to escape widening Communist power, he was committed to authentic Russian Orthodox spiritual traditions, but was to be overcome by the acrimonious infighting that constantly imperilled a church that existed at the ecclesiastical margins. When religious freedom returned to Russia – a land he never visited – he joined a new-founded jurisdiction that failed to gain the impetus he believed it might achieve.

He was born in 1926 in Serbia into a Russian noble family of Swedish origin which was also prominent in the Russian Orthodox Church. His father, Yuri Grabbe, was for many years right-hand man to the three earliest bishops of the Russian Orthodox Church outside Russia (ROCOR). Taking the name Grigory, Yuri would later become a priest and bishop, a path his son would follow.

The young Grabbe attended a Russian cadet school in the Serbian town of Bela Crkva until it was closed by the Nazis. After transferring to a Russian grammar school in Belgrade, he was conscripted in 1943 into the Vlasov army, a pro-Nazi and anti-Bolshevik force made up of Russians and former Soviet citizens, where he served in Andrei Vlasov's bodyguard.

As war ended, he was sent to a prisoner-of-war camp but was rescued by his younger brother Dmitry before he could suffer deportation by the Western powers into Stalin's clutches and imprisonment or execution. The two made their way to Munich, then under American control, where their father had transferred the Church's headquarters and archives to escape Tito's Communist takeover of Yugoslavia.

Anthony joined the newly founded St Job's monastery in Munich, and it was there in December 1948 – still only 22 – he was tonsured a monk. Like so many exiled Russians, he immigrated to the United States, where Russian Orthodoxy was long established. From 1949 to 1954 he studied at the Holy Trinity seminary in Jordanville, a major centre for the émigré Russian church, and was ordained a priest-monk at the end of his studies.

Father Anthony took on a variety of roles over the years, as secretary to ROCOR's leader, Archbishop Vitaly Maksimenko, head of the Jordanville monastery chancellery, and priest of the diocesan cathedral in New York. There he founded the St Sergius School, which he headed for nearly three decades.

After a sumptuous lunch over coffee, Father Anthony asked Andres to take me to his office in the Cathedral of the Mother of God of the Sign.[21]

The cathedral turned out to be the converted ballroom of a great house that once belonged to the Vanderbilt family. The rest of the house had become the headquarters of the Russian Orthodox New York diocese and, very importantly, also housed the St Sergius High School. Father Anthony was both administrator of the cathedral and

---

21   75 E 93rd St., New York

headmaster of the school. I remember well the fascinating day I spent visiting the classrooms and meeting the children and the nuns who taught them, before attending Vespers in the cathedral church where I was finally introduced to Bishop George Grabbe, Anthony's famous father.

Bishop George presented me with a beautiful silver cross studded with black agate stones and told me it had been presented to him, as a boy, by Tsar Nicholas at Livadia in the Crimea.

From that time, my friendship with Father Anthony and also with Andres, and later his beautiful Polish wife Lola, developed apace, and we kept closely in touch.

In 1968 Anthony was appointed head of the Russian Ecclesiastical Mission in Jerusalem and the Orthodox Society of Palestine. For the next fifteen years, he was in charge of the key properties in the Holy Land in the care of the mission, which was founded during the Tsarist era.

He faced a bruising challenge trying to hold on to property in the face of encroachments by the Israeli and Soviet governments, often working in cohort. He even won a court case against the Israeli government which had illegally transferred ownership of the St Mary Magdalene convent on the Mount of Olives and other property to the Moscow Patriarchate. The Israeli state was forced to pay compensation of $7 million.

I was extremely excited when Anthony telephoned me from Jerusalem shortly after his appointment, inviting me to visit him as soon as possible. This I did, accompanied by Andres, a few months later.

Having witnessed the horrors of the Six-Day War (1967) which had destroyed most of the Old Arab Quarter of Eastern Jerusalem and utterly changed its character (or so it seemed to me), I was pleasantly surprised to find the headquarters of the Russian Ecclesiastical Mission in Debagah Street in the midst of the Old Town in perfect shape. The impressive building had been purchased by the Imperial Orthodox Palestine Society under the patronage of Grand Duchess Elizabeth, sister of Alexandra and wife of Nicholas II. Internally it had all the appearance of an Imperial Palace, furnished throughout with fine

(French) furniture and numerous portraits of Russian notables, including several Tsars and Tsarinas.

Fortunately, the recent war had done little damage to the Christian holy sites, and I enjoyed visiting them in an environment of at least temporary peace. I made my first visit to the Bethany Community of the Resurrection, where I met the Abbess Maria, a delightful Scottish woman, and her deputy Vavara, daughter of a Muscovite banker. They, together with Father Anthony, took me along a winding path down from the Mount of Olives to the beautiful Church of St Mary Magdalene to pay homage at the shrine of Grand Duchess (now Saint) Elizabeth. After the murder of the royal family, the body of the Grand Duchess was found by the White Army, carried to Peking by a monk, and taken by sea to the Holy Land, where it was laid, as she had wished, in the church in Gethsemane. Her portrait hung in Abbess Maria's salon, dressed in her specially designed white nun's habit.

I was also taken by Anthony to the first of several audiences with the Greek Orthodox Patriarch of Jerusalem Benedictus. The audiences always ended with a small glass of local liquor served with rich Arabic coffee. On one occasion, an English friend thanked the Patriarch profusely for "the lovely Turkish coffee"! Greeks and Turks are not famous for their love of each other, and the Patriarch was not amused!

Most memorable of all my visits to Jerusalem with Father Anthony was Easter 1971, where I witnessed the phenomenon of the Holy Fire. This is known as "the Greatest of all Christian miracles". It takes place every year at the same time and in the same manner. One can read about it in sources from the eighth century AD. The miracle happens in the Church of the Holy Sepulchre in Jerusalem. The church itself is an enigmatic place. Theologians, historians, and archaeologists consider it to contain both Golgotha, the little hill on which Jesus Christ was crucified, as well as the "new tomb" close to Golgotha that received his dead body, as one reads in the Gospels. It is on this same spot that Christians believe he rose from the dead. It is known in the Orthodox world as the Church of the Resurrection.

One can trace the miracle throughout the centuries in the many itineraries to the Holy Land. The Russian Abbot Daniel in his itinerary, written in the years 1106-7, refers to the "Miracle of the Holy Light" and the ceremonies that frame it. He recalls how the Patriarch goes into the Sepulchre-chapel (the Anastasis) with two candles. The Patriarch kneels in front of the stone on which Christ was laid after his death and says certain prayers. Light proceeds from the core of the stone – a blue, indefinable light, which after some time kindles closed oil lamps, as well as the two candles of the Patriarch. This light is the Holy Fire, and it spreads to all people present in the church.

In order to be as close to the tomb as possible, pilgrims camp around the tomb-chapel, waiting from Holy Friday afternoon in anticipation of the wonder on Holy Saturday.

From around 11 a.m. Christian Arabs sing traditional songs. These songs date back to the Turkish occupation of Jerusalem in the thirteenth century, a period in which Christians were not allowed to sing their songs anywhere but in churches. "We are the Christians, this we have been for centuries, and this we shall be forever and ever. Amen!" they sing at the top of their voices, accompanied by the sound of drums. At 1 p.m. the songs fade out and there is silence, a tense and loaded silence electrified by the anticipation of the great manifestation of a phenomenon that all are about to witness.

At 1 p.m. a delegation of the local authorities elbows its way through the crowds. Even though these officials are not Christian, they are part of the ceremonies. In the times of the Turkish occupation of Palestine, they were Moslem Turks; today they are Israelis. Their function is to represent the Romans in the time of Jesus. The Gospels speak of the Romans who went to seal the tomb of Jesus, so his disciples would not steal his body and claim he had risen. In the same way, the Israeli authorities on this Easter Saturday come and seal the tomb with wax. Before they seal the door, it is customary that they enter the tomb to check for any hidden source of fire that could produce the miracle through fraud, just as the Romans were to guarantee that there was no manipulation after the death of Jesus.

When the tomb has been checked and sealed, the whole Church chants *Kyrie Eleison*. At 1.45 p.m. the Patriarch enters.

It is not possible to follow the events inside the tomb, so I pressed Father Anthony, who had previously questioned the Patriarch, about them. The Patriarch had told him:

I enter the tomb and kneel in front of the place where Christ lay after his death before his resurrection.

Then I find my way through the darkness towards the inner chamber, in which I fall on my knees. Here I say certain prayers that have been handed down to us through the centuries and, having said them, I wait. Sometimes I may wait a few minutes, but normally the miracle happens immediately after I have said the prayers. From the core of the very stone on which Jesus laid an indefinable light pours forth. It usually has a blue tint, but the colour may change and take many different hues. It cannot be described in human terms. The light rises out of the stone as mist may rise out of a lake. It almost looks as if the stone is covered by a moist cloud, but it is light. This light each year behaves differently. Sometimes it covers just the stone, while other times it gives light to the whole sepulchre, so that people who stand outside the tomb and look into it will see it filled with light. The light does not burn, and I have never had my beard burnt in all the years I have been Patriarch in Jerusalem and have received the Holy Fire. The light is of a different consistency than the normal fire that burns in an oil lamp.

At a certain point the light rises and forms a column in which the fire is of a different nature, so that I am able to light my candles from it. When I thus have received the flame on my candles, I go out and give the fire first to the Armenian Patriarch and then to the Coptic. Hereafter I give the flame to all people present in the church.

To believers this remarkable event is a miracle, and as all miracles, is surrounded by unexplainable factors. As Father Anthony explained:
Miracles cannot be proved. Faith is required, without which there is no miracle in the strict sense. The fire miracle has only one purpose – to extend the Grace of God in creation, and God cannot extend his Grace without faith on the part of his creatures. Therefore, there can be no miracle without faith.

In 1973 Father Anthony visited me in Norfolk, during which time he met Bridget Astor,[22] a brilliant horsewoman and keen professional photographer. At the time, Bridget's father Gavin[23] owned *The Times* newspaper. Anthony soon persuaded Bridget to visit Jerusalem for a photographic as well as spiritual pilgrimage, and in 1974 Bridget, Bronwen Astor[24] with a friend, John Wright, and I set off for a memorable visit.

As previously stated, a major preoccupation of Father Anthony whilst he was head of the Mission was to safeguard the properties belonging to the Russian Orthodox Church Abroad. Constant legal advice, lobbying, and international PR were vital, and with the latter Bridget proved to be an invaluable collaborator through her father and his colleagues at *The Times*.

Soon after his return to the United States, Anthony was forced out of his various positions after rumours of financial scandal. After a disagreement with the ROCOR leadership and failed attempts to re-forge links with the Serbian Orthodox Church, he joined the Greek True Orthodox jurisdiction, which consecrated him bishop in New York in 1996.

However, he soon retired and was scarcely active as a bishop. In 2001 he joined the Russian Orthodox Autonomous Church, led from the Russian town of Suzdal by Bishop Valentin. It had broken away from ROCOR after complaining of pro-Fascist sympathies among ROCOR's followers and moves to re-join the Moscow Patriarchate. Valentine's church recognized the validity of Anthony's consecration, and at his death he was the oldest of the Church's bishops.

I lost touch with Father Anthony soon after his return to America. Andres made two visits to Norfolk, bringing me some news of him, but about the same time Lola died, and soon after Andres followed her.

Clearly, Father Anthony's later life was far removed from the brilliance of his most fulfilling years in Jerusalem and New York. Immaculately turned out, superbly organized, a brilliant communicator

---

22 The Hon. Bridget Mary Smith, nee Astor (born 1948)
23 Gavin Astor, 2nd Baron Astor of Hever (1918–1984) was a British soldier, publisher, and peer.
24 Bronwen Astor, Viscountess Astor (born 1930), forerunner of today's supermodels.

and socially at ease, he would have excelled in most positions in his prime.

I am sorry that he did not live to see the formal reunification of the Russian Church Abroad, to which he had devoted his best years, and the Mother Church, now freed from its communist prison, but then understandably so abhorred by Anthony and his "white" contemporaries. If he had been in his prime now, he would have fitted perfectly into the sophisticated court of His Holiness Patriarch Kiril.

6: Anthony Gurney

Major Anthony Gurney

There have been Gurneys in Norfolk from time immemorial. In the rich mythology of local life, they played a leading role in the so-called "Norfolk Mafia", together with their cousins, the Buxtons and Barclays.

According to Anthony Gurney, in ancient times they were smugglers terrorizing the north Norfolk coast until their ill-gotten gains enabled them to integrate into the rural community. Other sources, mostly nineteenth century, reveal less exotic origins. Augustus Hare states that the family originated from Gournay in Normandy and that they were part of that French invasion of Old Saxon England which followed the Battle of Hastings in 1066, leading to the demise of the "English" monarchy forever.[25]

By the time that John Joseph Gurney was writing his family history, the Gurneys had become wealthy, partly through sheep farming at the time that the northern wool industry was flourishing. They also espoused a new form of Christianity known as the Quakers.[26] So fervent were they that the northern wool merchants trusted them completely with all the profits of their trade, and thus Gurney's Bank (later to become Barclays Bank) evolved in Norwich.

Newly rich, the Gurneys rented some of the grand houses of the local aristocracy until by the nineteenth century they were rich enough to buy great estates for themselves, and Gilbert and Sullivan were able to proclaim "as rich as the Gurneys".[27]

---

25 *The Gurneys of Earlham* (two volumes) by Augustus Hare, published by George Alben in 1895.
26 Also known as *The Society of Friends*
27 From the Judge's Song in *Trial by Jury* – words by Sir William Gilbert (1836–1911), music by Sir Arthur Sullivan (1842–1900).

This combination of religious fervour and enormous wealth produced some remarkable characters, most famous of whom was Elizabeth Fry,[28] the great prison reformer.

Almost as notable was Thomas Fowell Buxton,[29] a member of Parliament who championed the anti-slavery cause, following in the footsteps of William Wilberforce.[30] Once in Free Town, Sierra Leone, I dusted down an old statue of this champion of liberty, upon which was inscribed "Sir Thomas Fowell Buxton, M.P., Friend of the Negro".

Thus, from beautiful remote rural Norfolk emerged a dynasty of powerful bankers of social conscience dedicated to good works both within the local community and the wider world.

No one epitomizes these characteristics more than Anthony Gurney of Northrepps Manor Farm near Cromer. Larger than life and towering above lesser mortals, he typifies truly "Vintage Gurney".[31] Striding into life with unabashed enthusiasm and determination, he was always an example to aspiring young men and a great inspiration to me when setting out to conquer the world in my twenties.

Anthony was of that generation of Englishmen who, speaking loudly and confidently, expected and received both immediate attention and swift compliance to their wishes wherever they were in the world. They were men of Empire, where English opened every door and other languages were superfluous. But not entirely, for men of Anthony's calibre could quickly grasp a local language or dialect if it served their purpose, and I was not astounded to hear him converse with local Indians in Urdu, in spite of the fact that they understood English perfectly well. It was plain courtesy, you see, and courtesy and good manners were part of the very fabric of the British Empire way of life.

However far they roam, an Englishman's home is always his castle, and it was at home at Manor Farm that Anthony was in his element. A

---

28 Elizabeth Fry, nee Gurney (1780–1845) was an English prison reformer, social reformer and, as a Quaker, a Christian philanthropist.
29 Sir Thomas Fowell Buxton, 1st Baronet (1786–1845) was an English member of Parliament, abolitionist, and social reformer.
30 William Wilberforce (1759–1833) was a British politician, a philanthropist, and a leader of the movement to abolish the slave trade.
31 This phrase was first used by Bishop Aubrey Aitken at the memorial service for Anthony's cousin, Richard Quintin Gurney in Norwich Cathedral on May 29th in 1980.

log fire always burning, fresh flowers from the garden, the grand piano covered with family photographs, large, heavy portraits of ancestors, and comfortable chintz sofas provided the setting. A host of family dogs barking an enthusiastic greeting and our perpetual host organizing every conceivable drink provided the welcome to his lucky guests – a mixture of family and friends from near and far. For Anthony made friends in all corners of the world and all were welcomed to Northrepps.

The element of surprise has always been in the air with Anthony. One evening Patricia[32] was quietly watching television, Anthony being away in London, when a couple turned up in evening dress announcing that they had come to dinner. They had impressed Anthony during a train journey to the extent that he had spontaneously invited them for a dinner party. The only problem was that he had forgotten all about it! Luckily a good sense of humour prevailed as they sat over a boiled egg with Patricia in the kitchen.

Anthony's brother Joe,[33] the elder son, had inherited Northrepps Hall and most of the land around it, leaving Anthony with the more modest Manor Farm and the challenge of making his own way in the world. This he most successfully did by gradually building up a substantial farming enterprise with the help of Patricia, who developed a famous herd of cattle. Buyers of the cattle came from all over the world, including the late Shah of Persia.

Much of this success has resulted from Anthony's communicative skills and naturally gregarious manner.

Long before Perestroika, Anthony was in Russia visiting remote collective farms. Defying all bureaucracy, he invited a thirty-strong delegation of Soviet farmers to Northrepps (in 1978). I was lucky to be there, and no one present could forget the occasion. A few phrases of quickly learned Russian, a quick round of gins and tonics, and the party relaxed to enjoy a superb tour of Anthony's estate – then at the height of its success – sitting on bales of straw on tractor-drawn carts, followed by excited dogs and curious farm workers.

After their first experience of capitalist farming, the party tucked into a sumptuous feast washed down by endless glasses of wine and

---

32 Patricia Gurney, nee Shaw, Anthony's wife.
33 Joseph Gurney (1914–2001)

thoughtfully provided vodka, before heading back to Heathrow airport and home. English-Russian relations were certainly enhanced by this agricultural initiative.

A large picture hangs in the front hall of Manor Farm. It is entitled *The King's Butt*.[34] It is a typical highland scene of a wild grouse moor, painted from behind the artificial and well camouflaged cover behind which generations of "guns" have waited in excited expectation of challenging sport.

Anthony had been patiently standing in that very butt one late summer's day awaiting the first drive. Suddenly he sensed a presence behind him, and he turned to see a small woman in a mackintosh and floppy hat. It was the Queen Mother.

Quietly she said, "Don't let me disturb you, Major Gurney. This was my husband's favourite spot".[35]

So surprised was Anthony by this unexpected presence (not so surprising in retrospect, as it was on her own estate[36]) that he missed each fast flying bird. This disappointment, however, was more than compensated for as he had found a new and fascinating friend.

Next day, driving south, Anthony stopped at an antique shop in Ballater, wherein he found the picture.

A few weeks later, admiring the picture in its place of honour in the front hall, Anthony made a decision: he would invite Her Majesty to visit Manor Farm to see the picture of that place which had meant so much to her husband. Lady Angela Oswald, a friend and neighbour, was lady-in-waiting to Queen Elizabeth[37] and assured Anthony that she would pass on the invitation.

To Anthony's great pleasure, a telephone call the following December from Lady Angela brought the good news that Her Majesty had accepted the invitation and would be delighted to lunch at Manor Farm the following week.

---

34 Grouse butts (from the Gaelic word *buta*) are small, wood, stone, and turf constructions used to give cover to keepers and shooters – "Guns".
35 King George VI, Albert Frederick Arthur George (1895–1952)
36 Brikhall
37 As the Queen Mother was known, to distinguish her from her daughter, Her Majesty the Queen.

There followed a flurry of activity. Despite the winter gloom, everything was "spring cleaned", and even the lawn, under a light sprinkling of frost, was mown. Extra cooks were hired and the farm workers rehearsed in the formalities of welcoming a Queen.

"And don't forget to put out your filthy woodbines as Her Majesty approaches," commanded Anthony to his somewhat bewildered men.

The great day arrived. Her Majesty appeared and with her natural charm and kindness immediately put all at ease.

Christopher Gurney[38] recalls bringing up the subject of Rhodesia[39] over lunch and then realizing that political correctness required its new name!

"It will always be Rhodesia to me," immediately responded the reassuring voice of Her Majesty.

The Royal patience was only once slightly tested when, despite all the redecoration, the loo door handle failed to work. A diplomatic knocking soon brought a somewhat embarrassing rescue.

Thereafter, the Queen Mother's visits became regular events during her Christmas visits to nearby Sandringham.

Very regularly, Anthony left Norfolk for London.

"Up to London for a couple of days," he would announce to Patricia, who rather relished the tranquillity that suddenly replaced the constant comings and goings when Anthony was at home.

Changing into his dark city suit and clutching his ancient attaché case, Anthony strode into the dining car of the 8 a.m. train from Norwich to London. Over many years, the dining car had become an extension of numerous Norfolk dining rooms, and almost everyone knew each other. Thus, the London party began almost before the train had left Norfolk. Sumptuous breakfasts of kippers, kedgeree, bacon, and eggs were the order of the day in those more civilized times.

Upon arrival in the great metropolis, Anthony was well fortified to begin an onerous round of meetings – the bank (Barclays, of course), the stockbroker, and Lloyds (for underwriting) – all to be fitted in before dashing off to Boodles for a splendid lunch of oysters in season[40] or

---

38 Anthony's eldest son.
39 Now known as Zimbabwe.
40 Only in those months containing an R.

lobster, roast beef, and a heavy pudding – and, of course, in those days before the bureaucratic tentacles of the sinister EU had reached into the bosom of old England, cigars.

Refortified by lunch, Anthony would dash into Hatchards for the latest biography, look into an art exhibition, and end up dropping into Clarence House for a cup of tea with Sir Martin Gilliat[41] – that is if the Queen Mother was not at home to welcome him.

Anthony belonged to several dining clubs, without doubt, his favourite being the Foxhunters. Into this august body he had introduced me in the early 1980s. It was a sight that evoked eighteenth century splendour – a table surrounded by country men in white tie and hunt coats, tucking into several delicious courses washed down by a variety of fine wines, interspersed by numerous toasts, most importantly "To Foxhunting", and the nostalgic sound of the hunting horn, all in flickering candle light "going home … going home".[42] But not quite yet to bed – final drinks at Boodles or even Annabel's, and possibly other unmentionable delights.

All his life Anthony had thrived on travelling, especially to far-flung places. Part of his war had been spent in South Asia – India, Malaya, and Burma, where he had found a number of rubies which he temporally (or so he thought) had concealed in a temple compound. Returning after the enemy had devastated Rangoon, Anthony searched for but could not find the rubies, but he did find a small beautifully sculptured figure of Buddha which today graces his dining room.

A happy luncheon in that room many years later was attended by the late President J.R. Jayewardene of Sri-Lanka,[43] a Buddhist himself, who was fascinated to see this symbol of his faith in rural England.

Dinners at Anthony's table could never be dull, for he not only has an endless stream of real life dramas to relate but is also an expert in getting others to do the same.

On July 19 2000, the Queen Mother celebrated her hundredth birthday with a magnificent three-hour parade at Horse Guards. Anthony first invited me to lunch at Boodles, before we walked into

---

41   Private Secretary to Her Majesty (1913–1993) working for H.M. 1956–1993.
42   *Going home* – the final blowing of the horn at the end of a day's foxhunting.
43   See chapter 18

the stand to find our places just behind the two thrones prepared for Queen Elizabeth and Prince Charles. We were so close that we were able to hear the Prince gently suggest that his grandmother sit down.

"I will not sit whilst my regiments pass by," was her retort, which meant that we all had to constantly rise, including Anthony with great effort as he was recovering from a major leg operation, while Her Majesty's regiments paraded by and stopped for each salute.

It was gloriously, riotously, eccentrically British. Soldiers, pensioners, camels, horses, children in fancy dress, and men in fancy hats rode, danced, marched, and capered in front of a rapt old lady, pretty in pink and often waving, seated on her throne – a cross between an exotic palanquin and a garden gazebo – as the sun's rays set on Horse Guards Parade but not, it seemed, on the Empire over which she and her husband once reigned.

After rising for the National Anthem for the final time, Anthony and I joined the vast throng singing with gusto:

Here's a health unto Her Majesty,
With a fa la la la la la la la,
Confusion to her enemies,
With a fa la la la la la la la,
And he who would not drink her health,
We wish him neither wit nor wealth.
Nor yet a rope to hang himself,
With a fa la la la la la la la la …[44]

The Queen Mother left in her open coach and we on foot through the spellbound crowd.

"Splendid," said Anthony. "Quite splendid."

---

44 Traditional English song by Jeremy Saville, 1650.

7: Victor Bristol

Victor Frederick Cochrane Hervey, 6th Marquess of Bristol

I first met Victor when I was in my mid-twenties. I was introduced to him by Joe Gurney[45] who had known him for many years and was both amused by him and in awe of him. He regaled me with tales of exotic banquets at Ickworth,[46] where food was served on gold plates which were surrounded by a multitude of glasses – at least eight per place – of the finest crystal, perpetually filled with finest vintage wines by elegant footmen – one per guest. Above all, Joe recalled the scores of beautiful women, many hoping to be Victor's next wife or even mistress.

I yearned to experience this fantastic scene for myself and was amazed to receive an invitation to a shoot at Ickworth – almost certainly engineered by Joe, who, I think, rather relished the thought of this novice shot, a one-gun man, plunged into the grandest of sporting occasions! My experience of shooting thus far had been confined to Norfolk shoots with one gun and certainly no loaders.[47]

Victor did not shoot himself (anyway not on that occasion), but he strode about, the perfect host, dressed in an immaculate grey suit with a striking tie held in place by a gold tie pin bearing his coronet. Thus he presided over the draw. Just as I had drawn third peg, Victor rushed over to introduce me to his guest who had drawn the fourth peg.

"You have met His Majesty before?"

I had not. This was quickly remedied, and I found myself in conversation with Simeon Saxe-Coburg-Gotha, King of the Bulgarians.

---

45 Joseph Gurney of Northrepps Hall, Norfolk (1914–2001)
46 Ickworth Park, Suffolk.
47 At the grandest shoots "loaders" were provided if one did not have one's own "man", who stood behind you quickly handing over the second gun after the second cartridge had been fired.

During the several intervals between drives I had fascinating discussions with Simeon, who had been crowned in Sophia Cathedral as a child before being taken into exile by his mother, Queen Joanna.[48] He ended up as a very successful property magnate in Spain.[49]

Long before the demise of communism in his native land, he had remarkable secret meetings with "commissars" in neutral Switzerland, where he was impressed that they not only exercised all courtesy but all addressed him as "Your Majesty". Perhaps they possessed prophetic insight.

A royal guest at Ickworth was not unusual, for royalty was at the centre of Victor's life. Over a sumptuous lunch, sitting close to my host, he spoke of the Monarchist League, of which he had recently been elected Chancellor. He invited me to join the League, which I did a few days later, and within another couple of weeks he invited me to lunch in London to talk more about it.

Victor could be both charming and persuasive, and on this occasion he was both. By the time we were well into the port, he had convinced me that he could only cope with his duties as Chancellor if I assisted him. And thus I found myself appointed to the illustrious position of Principal Secretary and Receiver General. The only downside, I quickly discovered, was that I had to provide my own assistant secretaries and that there were few funds to receive!

However, all was well as I had plenty of time (in those days), an under-employed secretary, and reasonable resources. In fact, Victor also discovered that the League was broke (a huge amount of money had disappeared under the former regime) and that he was expected to subsidize it to a very considerable extent. For example, the League had an annual banquet for "regnant and non-regnant" monarchs (who were also mostly "down and out"), their retinues, and other members. Some hundred or more attended these feasts, heralded by trumpeters from various regiments, entertained by string quartets, feasting on course after delicious course, washed down by fine wines, champagne, cognacs, finest Cuban cigars. The ladies were dressed in regal gowns

---

48 Queen Joanna (1907–2000) former Princess Giovanna of Italy, House of Savoy.
49 Later His Majesty was uniquely elected as prime minister of Bulgaria 2001–2009.

and glittering tiaras, the men in uniform, levee dress, or white tie with orders and decorations.

All was paid for by Victor, and he enjoyed every moment of it. Yes, some journalists described it all as Ruritanian, and it certainly was both amusing and entertaining. However, there was a deadly serious side.

Almost all royalty present had lost their loved ones in revolutions and were survivors of an old order that had been almost entirely destroyed between the assassination of Franz-Ferdinand[50] in 1914 and the murder of the Romanovs shortly to follow.[51] Others from Middle Eastern and African countries had suffered similar fates. Victor's royal banquets at the Savoy Hotel gave them nostalgic memories – perhaps even a form of extended and unconscious mourning – and therefore some consolation.

This was in the 1970s and 1980s when it was only just dawning on some perceptive souls that parliamentary democracy, often led by self-seeking politicians, was not a panacea, and that monarchy, as Victor used to say, might be the "best policy", or at least, constitutional Monarchy. He often referred to the successful example of the accession of King Juan Carlos in Spain, smoothly taking over from the Franco dictatorship.

Despite the fact that few monarchs were destined to return to their thrones, several were destined to play an important role in their countries, including Simeon in Bulgaria, Crown Prince Alexander in Serbia, and King Michael in Rumania.

The Monarchist League, under Victor's leadership, played an important role in encouraging the royal cause in a modern world – encouragement through innumerable letters, telegrams, and telephone calls, and the organization of regional seminars. In fact, by the time of his death thriving branches of the League existed in Canada, Australia, New Zealand, Germany, and (somewhat underground) in Russia even during the final communist years.

Somehow Victor had developed an instinct that monarchy was not dead but, on the contrary, would be on the ascendency again. He seems to have been right. Only this year (2010), Grand Duchess Maria was

---

50 Franz Ferdinand (1863–1914) was an Archduke of Austria-Este, Austro-Hungarian and Royal Prince of Hungary and of Bohemia.
51 The Russian Royal Family was murdered in Yekaterinburg on 17 July 1918.

the first to receive Easter communion from the Patriarch in Moscow's revived Cathedral of Christ the King, taking precedence over both President and Premier!

I did not know Victor in his "colourful days[52]" when he was the preoccupation of the gutter press for so many years – the Mayfair Gang, sinister connections, and a prison sentence. Thus I could not possibly comment. However, taking into account the undoubted truth of Shakespeare's words, "The evil that men do lies after them, the good is oft interred with their bones",[53] I prefer to dwell on the "good" that I found in Victor.

And there was quite a lot.

Above all he was a loyal friend. He was of that old vintage of men whose bond of friendship was more important than any other factor, including disgrace, impropriety, and law-breaking. Such characters know nothing of fair-weather friends.

He could get very drunk, but as is well observed, excessive drink tends to bring out true character: the moronic appear more so, and the colourful exceedingly so. Victor was therefore never offensive when drunk, just a little more colourful and humorous (despite any underlying despair).

During his final years in London, out of a much reduced staff there remained the faithful butler Batt. Upon my arrival, he would pour me a very large whisky, and for Victor an awful non-alcoholic drink called Tab. As soon as Batt left the room, Victor would down my whisky in one gulp, leaving me with the Tab (which is how I know it is awful). Victor would then ring the bell, and an astonished Batt would appear to refill the glasses. This would happen two or three times, which is why *I* got the reputation, in that household, of being an alcoholic.

Thus fortified, Victor would lead me, gasping for a real drink, to the Silver Shadow Rolls Royce in which we were driven to only the very best of restaurants. Good English food was also Victor's motto. Perhaps best of all was the un-modernized dining room at Claridge's, where we would tuck into a dozen oysters (in season) with champagne, followed

---

52   As described in a recent UK television programme *The Real Pink Panther* TV 2009.
53   From *Julius Caesar* by William Shakespeare.

by beef and kidney pudding, with a good claret being the only foreign concession. Vintage port came with a cigar, and although Victor had given up smoking years before, being the perfect host, he always insisted that I have one. This became very difficult in his final years when he was stricken with emphysema as, naturally, I did not wish to smoke. Still he would insist, so after one small puff, I would let the cigar go out hoping he would not notice.

It was during these long lunches that we would discuss art. Or rather, Victor would instruct and I would listen. Art was high on his list of enthusiasms, especially watercolour painting, of which genre he was an expert. He introduced me to Alma-Tadema[54] whose vivid azure skies provided the perfect setting for shining white marble columns and languorous Grecian ladies. He kindled in me a passion for English watercolour and encouraged me to start my own collection. Not only did he have an aesthetic appreciation of those pictures but also a practical skill in their acquisition. He had a good eye and helped me develop mine. And he knew a bargain. One of his tips was to visit an art fair on the first day just to view and make a mental note of something interesting. Then to return on the final day when the tired exhibitors were only too happy to give a huge discount – sometimes, Victor told me, as much as fifty per cent.

Victor was a compulsive collector. And he also had a keen eye for presentation. These two aspects combined to produce the opulent interiors of Ickworth and his London homes. Though he had inherited a good deal of furniture and some notable paintings, the majority of the contents displayed to pleasing effect were of his own choice and reflected his own impeccable taste. Elegant and comfortable rooms packed with *objets d'art*, eighteenth-century (mostly French) furniture, portraits, watercolours, books, and flowers are the epitome of the English style which Victor relished. He taught me that one did not need enormous wealth to create such an ambiance – a good eye, presentational skill, and a natural sense of balance were the essential ingredients.

For instance, though most rooms contained some original old master paintings, they were intermingled with perfect (but inexpensive)

---

54 Sir Lawrence Alma-Tadema OM, RA (1836–1912) was one of the most renowned painters of late nineteenth-century Britain.

twentieth-century copies, and most guests would never know the difference. Clearly Victor had no need of professional interior designers. He could have taught *them* a thing or two!

Perhaps Victor should have been a novelist. He told many a good story, embellished to great effect as time rolled on. Most memorable were his tales of the Lima treasure in the Cocos Islands.

The Lima treasure is the most famous and valuable of all the treasures reputedly hidden on Cocos Island. While Simon Bolivar marched through Peru in 1823, a group of Spaniards in Lima "liberated" what was probably the Peruvian state treasure. To get it out of South America, they put it on board the *Mary Dier* under the command of a Scotsman, William Thompson. A partial bill of lading included 113 gold religious statues, mostly of Catholic saints, 200 chests of jewels, 250 swords with jewelled hilts, 150 chalices, 300 bars of gold, and 600 bars of silver. A bishop, the governor of Lima, and some other Spaniards went aboard to keep the treasure company, an error they paid for with their lives. Overcome with greed, Captain Thompson and his crew killed them. Thompson, now a pirate, sailed to Cocos, where it is said he stashed the treasure in a cave. As the *Mary Dier* left the island, however, it was attacked and captured by the Spanish frigate *Espiegle*. Thompson and a member of his crew were taken to the island under duress to lead their captors to the treasure, but the wily Scotsmen escaped and hid. After a fruitless search for the treasure, the *Espiegle* weighted anchor and left. A month later, the crew of a whaler that had stopped at Cocos for fresh water found Thompson, who said that his companion had died. Thompson never returned to the island, but he gave his friend John Keating a chart and detailed information about where the treasure had been hidden.

It is believed that Keating and a companion rediscovered the treasure but withheld the knowledge from the crew of their ship. The crew, suspecting what was going on, promptly mutinied. The two escaped to the island and hid. Now Keating's story parallels Thompson's. He was rescued by a whaler and reported that his companion had died. He too failed to return to the island, and he entrusted his secret to a friend. He had, however, left the island with about £3,000 in gold.

If My Table Could Talk

In 1872 Thomas Welsh and his wife – leaders of the South Pacific Treasure Island Prospecting Company – and several of their followers dug an eighty-foot tunnel into a mountain, at the end of which, they claimed, lay $65 million in gold. It took them eight days, and they found nothing. After soothing his enraged helpers, Welsh had them dig 200 feet further into the mountain, a twelve-day job, which still netted them no gold.

Somehow the secret of the treasure was passed down to Victor, who passed the document headed "top secret" on to me! He told me stories of his own attempt to find it – the stuff of legend – but all to no avail. Again sensing he was close to success, his crew also attempted mutiny, paying for their disloyalty, said Victor, "with bullets in the back of their heads." He came home, as others before, with nothing more than entertaining tales to tell.

Victor, happily married to Yvonne[55] and the proud father of three children all born when he was in his sixties, spent his final years in Monte Carlo.

I visited him there occasionally and did not feel he *really* relished life there despite outward appearances. His thoughts often returned to England and the old days, never to return, at "Sweet Ickworth".[56] Of course, though it was much smaller than he had been used to, his apartment was beautifully and elegantly appointed, and there was another butler and now also a nanny. It was his old friends he missed most.

"We entertain people here who would not be seen dead in an English drawing room," he remarked to me one day. Images of shady characters arose, wearing heavy gold bracelets and hiding behind dark glasses – shades of Gatsby?

Then a wink, a smile – and out to a sumptuous lunch.

---

55 Yvonne, Marchioness of Bristol, nee Sutton (born 1945) married Victor in 1974.
56 Actually he did return twenty-five years later. On October 7 2010, his closest family and just a few old friends gathered at Ickworth to witness Victor's return to be finally laid to rest in the family vault where his ancestors have been buried since 1467.

8: John Glubb

General Sir John Bagot Glubb, KCB, CMG, DSO, OBE, MC – Glubb Pasha

It is those we meet in our formative years whose influence lasts longest. I was simply the luckiest young man to have Glubb Pasha[57] as an early mentor.

He taught me that when a desert Arab (Bedouin) looks you in the eye and shakes you firmly by the hand, he can be relied upon one hundred per cent. In English we say, "a gentleman's word is his bond," but this was perhaps even stronger.

Though he was by regiment a Royal Engineer his knowledge of intelligence, in an Arab context, was superior to any textbook.

In those valuable hours in 1966, before the horrors of the Six-Day War.[58] I felt I had created a rapport with the great man strong enough to embolden me, a few years later, to invite him to Norfolk.

By 1970 I was deeply involved in the Council for the Advancement of Arab-British Understanding – CAABU for short – leading its activities in East Anglia, of which Norwich in the county of Norfolk is the major city. It was felt that my experience in Palestine was of value in helping to develop awareness of Arabia in general and the increasingly sorry plight of the Palestinians in particular.

---

57 *Pasha* or *pacha*, was a high rank in the Ottoman Empire's political system, typically granted to governors, generals, and dignitaries. As an honorary title, *Pasha*, in one of its various ranks, is equivalent to the British title of Lord, and was also one of the highest titles in pre-republic Egypt.

58 *The Six-Day War* or *June War*, also known as the 1967 Arab-Israeli War or the Third Arab-Israeli War, was fought between June 5 and June 10 1967, by Israel and the neighbouring states of Egypt, known then as the United Arab Republic (UAR)], Jordan, and Syria.

Who better, I thought, to launch our initiative than the by then legendary Glubb Pasha?

Lieutenant-General Sir John Bagot Glubb was born in Lancashire in 1897. Educated at Cheltenham College, he was commissioned into the Royal Engineers in 1915. He was seriously wounded on the western front, his jaw being shattered. In later years this would lead to the Arab nickname of *abu Hunaik*, meaning "of the little jaw". He was transferred to Iraq in 1920, which was then governed by Britain according to the League of Nations Mandate. He became an officer of the Arab Legion in 1930. The next year he formed the Desert Patrol — a force consisting exclusively of Bedouins — to curb the raiding problem that plagued the southern part of the country. Within a few years he had persuaded the Bedouins to abandon their habit of raiding neighbouring tribes. In 1939, Glubb succeeded Frederick Peake[59] as the commander of the Arab Legion (now known as Jordan Royal Army). During this period, he transformed the legion into the best trained force in the Arab world.

During the 1948 Arab–Israeli War, the Arab legion was considered the strongest Arab army involved in the war. Glubb led the Arab Legion across Jordan to occupy the West Bank. Despite some negotiation and understanding between the Jewish Agency and King Abdullah, severe fighting took place in Kfar Etzion, Jerusalem, and Latrun.

Glubb remained in charge of the defence of the West Bank following the armistice in March 1949. He continued as the commander of the Arab Legion until 1 March 1956, when he was dismissed by King Hussein who wanted to distance himself from the British and disprove the contention of Arab nationalists that Glubb was the actual ruler of Jordan. Differences between Glubb and Hussein had been apparent since 1952, especially over defence arrangements, the promotion of Arab officers, and the funding of the Arab Legion. Despite his decommission, which was forced upon him by public opinion, he remained a close friend of the King.

The General responded warmly to my invitation to visit Norfolk and to address a public meeting under the auspices of CAABU in Norwich. To my great joy, he agreed to stay with us for a couple of days.

---

59 Major-General Frederick Gerard Peake (1886–1970) known as Peake Pasha, was a British Army and police officer and creator of the Arab Legion.

Word quickly got about that Glubb Pasha was to appear, and several hundred people turned up to hear him speak, which he did for over an hour without notes, in the Assembly House in Norwich. Alas, not only sympathizers appeared. A bus load of Zionist[60] supporters also drove from London, some of whom thought to outwit Glubb during question time, but they failed as he dealt with all their issues authoritatively, fairly, and courteously. Like many great soldiers, he was of gentle disposition, unaggressive with natural charm a chief component of his armoury. He also understood that the power of the word is greater than that of the sword.

Not only was he an eloquent and convincing speaker but also a competent and interesting writer. His command of English was second to none, as any who have read his books will attest.

The General had arrived by car during the afternoon before the meeting and to my astonishment, as well as his overnight case, he brought into the house a parcel of books – in fact all the books he had written to date![61] I was not only delighted to receive the books but also to find that he had carefully signed and dated each one – 8 June 1973. They have remained a treasured part of my library ever since.

Returning home from the exciting meeting, we dined late, retreating into the library at 11 p.m. Like me the General enjoyed whisky, and we drank a whole bottle into the early hours.

It is no exaggeration to say that those were some of the most fascinating hours of my life. I was privileged to share some of Glubb's amazing experiences first hand as he opened my imagination to the mysterious world of the orient, the desert, the Bedouin, and his way of life. It was easy to see why Glubb, like Lawrence,[62] enjoyed the trust

---

60 Zionism is a nationalist Jewish political movement that, in its broadest sense, calls for the self-determination of the Jewish people and a sovereign, Jewish national homeland.

61 Since his return from the Middle East he had concentrated on writing history and memoirs including: *The Yezidis, Sulubba, and Other Tribes of Iraq and Adjacent Regions*, 1943; *The Story of the Arab Legion*, 1948; *A Soldier with the Arabs*, 1957; *Britain and the Arabs: A Study of Fifty Years*, 1959; *War in the Desert: An R.A.F. Frontier Campaign*, 1960; *The Great Arab Conquests*, 1963; *The Empire of the Arab*, 1963; etc.

62 Lieutenant Colonel Thomas Edward Lawrence (1888–1935) known professionally as T. E. Lawrence, was a British Army officer renowned especially for his liaison

and loyalty of the proud Arabs for both men had entered into their very spirits and minds – and loved and respected them. I felt the long sweep of history pass before me as Glubb placed recent events into their context and explained what before had appeared inexplicable. He had a knack of simplifying things, and one felt that if only political leaders could have had his insight and understanding, peace would be possible.

I think we got to bed about 4 a.m. After a late breakfast, the great man set off for his home in Mayfield, Sussex warmly inviting me to stay with him if ever I was in those parts.

Sussex was not one of my usual stamping grounds, and time passed by with no communication until I received a letter from him in April 1975:[63]

> ...I have got a bit older since I visited you in Norwich and have not given any lectures for over a year. I'm afraid I shall probably not be able to come again, though I hope to feel better in the summer if the weather would stop snowing!
>
> I am so glad that your branch of CAABU is doing so well ...
>
> Let me know if there is any chance of your coming our way ...

This encouraged me to telephone Sir John, and a date was fixed for my visit later in the year. Subsequent telephone calls, however, made it clear that he was not well, and the visit was postponed for a few months more. In fact, a date was not set until late August 1976.

Just before leaving Norfolk, I decided to call again. To my surprise, the General answered the phone immediately, uncharacteristically shouting, "Don't come. I can't speak now!" End of conversation.

I was perplexed and worried. I decided not to ring again and await events.

---

role during the Arab Revolt against Ottoman Turkish rule of 1916–1918. He has earned international fame as Lawrence of Arabia, a title popularized by the 1962 film based on his life.

63 Letter from Sir John Glubb to Michael Wynne-Parker, 4 April 1975.

A few months later a letter arrived – four pages in the familiar handwriting. It was a letter of explanation and apology, well worthy of quoting almost in full:[64]

> ...Other people's ailments are a bore, but I'm afraid I must describe ours in order to explain to you what happened.
>
> My wife had a complaint called Mounier's Disease. This comes on periodically in sudden but very intense attacks of wild giddiness. The whole world flies round and round and all the patient can do is to lie with eyes closed on her bed. The giddiness results at the same time in violent attacks of vomiting. The result is agonizing for the patient and also for the onlooker. When she had an attack, I never could leave her bedside.
>
> It was on such an occasion that you telephoned. I was most anxious to see you, and asked her if I could leave her for a few moments, but she begged me so passionately not to leave her, that I could only tell you please not to come.
>
> You may say that I need not have waited so long to explain. The fact is that one night in September I suddenly woke up at 2 a.m. in a wild delirium. We afterwards discovered that my pacemaker had suddenly stopped owing to a mechanical fault, and my heart stopped with it. In a minute I should have been dead, when, as if by a miracle, my natural heart started up again, though it had been driven by a pacemaker for six years. But it could only manage thirty beats to the minute instead of seventy-two. No one round here has a pace-maker clinic. So they put me into an ambulance and drove madly to London. By 5 a.m. I was on the operating table, still just alive and spent four and a half hour on the table!
>
> This episode knocked me out for about four months, during which I slowly regained strength. My wife continued to have

---

64 Letter from Sir John Glubb to Michael Wynne-Parker, 17 May 1977.

giddy fits until the end of November. After that, thank God, the specialist produced a new drug and she has not had any more fits since the end of November.

I continued to be very unwell, and on 25th February I was admitted to the London Hospital and operated on for prostate gland. This was not nearly as bad as the heart failure, and we are both now much better.

Please excuse this long rigmarole, but I wanted to convince you that I have not changed, but have just been physically out of action.

Please drop me a line to tell me your news and that you have forgiven me …"

Naturally this letter made a lasting impression. Only a great man would take the time and trouble to write such a detailed letter to a young man.

One or two more meetings followed, the most notable at the General's Club, the Naval & Military – then called the In-and-Out – in Piccadilly. Over a good lunch, but not too much whisky this time, my mentor went into the historical background of the present Palestine-Israeli conflict, starting some five hundred years before Christ.

Many things were made clear to me for the first time, and after the luncheon I began to read perhaps the General's greatest book *Peace in the Holy Land* (a historical analysis of the Palestine problem) – one of the books he had given me. I completely agreed with *The Times* comment: "Sir John Glubb … as always a clear guide, illuminating history by the fruits of his own experience".[65]

A devout Christian, Glubb had clear and balanced views on Jerusalem. It was and always would be the spiritual centre for Jew, Christian, and Muslim equally. It must be administered by an independent authority made up of leading representatives of the three monotheistic religions. It should never be the capital of just one nation, but the cultural hub

---

65 *The Times*, 1971

of Arab and Jew alike. Synagogues, mosques, and churches should exist side by side, their worshipers exercising respect for all. Leaders of Glubb's calibre are needed all the more today to get this message across.

In Westminster Abbey on 17 April 1986 a large congregation assembled for Glubb Pasha's memorial service. It was a celebration as much as a remembrance, which began with the deposition of the great man's medals and decorations by his grandson Mubarak Glubb and an officer of the Hashemite Army, who wore the traditional red headdress in which Glubb had been seen many times in photographs that made him a figure of romance among the British public, to whom it brought echoes of Lawrence of Arabia. However, to the Bedouin of Syria and Jordan among whom he had served, Glubb had long been considered a greater man than Lawrence, said the General's biographer, Major General James Lunt[66] who gave the address.

The service came to a dramatic conclusion. After the final prayers there was an enormous clap of thunder, followed by a rustling sound through the microphones, before the distinctive voice of King Hussein[67] rang out in an impromptu speech. He spoke movingly of Glubb Pasha's profound impact on the Kingdom of Jordan and said he belonged to a unique generation of Englishmen who dedicated themselves to the Arab world.

> His retirement should have been the most natural of events, but regrettably the retirement became embroiled in the whirlwind of international politics. Yet the memory of Glubb Pasha lived in the hearts of the Jordanian people.

These were sincere and remarkable words from the King, who at the age of sixteen had been forced to dismiss him.

Leaving the Abbey in a mood of near ecstasy, I was quickly brought back to earth. The thunder storm was raging, rain was teeming down,

---

66 Major-General James Lunt (1917–2000) widely known as the biographer of two men under whom he had served, John Bagot Glubb 'Pasha' and King Hussein of Jordan.
67 His Majesty King Hussein bin Talal (1935–1999) was the King of Jordan from the abdication of his father, King Talal, in 1952, until his death.

and, of course, not a taxi anywhere. Everyone was searching, so I decided to make the best of it and walked towards the English Speaking Union Headquarters in Charles Street where I had a meeting. Soon, soaked to the skin, I realized I could not attend a meeting in that state, so I dived into a men's clothing shop nearby fifteen minutes before the meeting was due to begin.

"I need a jacket, trousers, shirt and dry underwear," I said to the astonished assistant as, to make the point, I began to strip off, water dripping everywhere. I was led into a small room and hurriedly changed into clothes that, amazingly, fitted perfectly. My shoes were dried, and ten minutes later I left the shop under a large umbrella and just made the meeting in time.

I think Glubb Pasha would have enjoyed that story!

9: Walter Walker

General Sir Walter Colyear Walker, KCB, CBE, DSO

There were spies everywhere. Prime Minister Wilson[68] presided over a disintegrating government. Rumours of a Soviet takeover of the BBC were taken seriously, and the trade unions were increasingly militant. A hero was desperately needed, but where was he to be found?

In July 1973 I received a telephone call from one Brigadier Graham.[69] He explained that he would like to meet me in private as soon as possible.

Intrigued, I agreed, and the Brigadier came to lunch the following day. He told me that he had been recruited as coordinator of Civil Assistance in Norfolk by its head, General Sir Walter Walker[70] and that I had been recommended to be his deputy. My duties? First, to make available a County Headquarters, and second, to help recruit suitable leaders of the community throughout the county.

Even more intrigued, I agreed again and made over a property in central Norwich, pledging also my time and influential contacts.

The name of the game was to identity trusted chaps in every village and town who were to be briefed and given bicycles and torches, and who were to be at the ready – but to be briefed and to be ready for what?

According to the Brigadier, for the Soviet invasion.

---

68 James Harold Wilson, Baron Wilson of Rievaulx (1916–1995) was a British Labour politician; he served two terms as prime minister of the United Kingdom, first from 1964 to 1970, and again from 1974 to 1976.
69 Brigadier Cyril Carew Graham, CBE,DSO (1907–1989)
70 General Sir Walter Colyear Walker, KCB, CBE, DSO (1912–2001)

On the wall of the Operations Room was a map of the county, and I began to identity connections and friends who would not be shocked to be told of the impending disruption of services by the unions that would lead to invasion by the Soviets.

Credibility, I thought, was the essence, and not all my friends would take this seriously. I expressed my misgivings to the Brigadier and he at once telephoned General Walker.

"My boy, the General understands and wishes to meet you at the first opportunity in London. He will answer all your questions and reassure you."

Thus I met the remarkable General Sir Walter Walker. He was charm personified.

"Come in, sit down, and relax. I have heard of your generous support. Let me explain all."

The General was handsome, dignified, and approachable, and without speaking, he commanded respect – a leader of men who had achieved more than most in his super active and illustrious career.

He was born on a tea plantation in British India to a military family, one of four sons. At the end of the First World War, his family moved back to Britain and he was sent to Blundell's School in Devon. Even as a child Walker had a militaristic streak; in his memoirs, *Fighting On*, he says he ordered the previously "idle, unpatriotic, unkempt" pupils into "showing the school what smartness on the parade ground meant." His teachers became alarmed at Walker's strict behaviour and tried to explain the difference between "driving" and "leading".

He then went to Sandhurst and in 1933, after a short attachment to the Sherwood Foresters, joined his grandfather's regiment, the 1/8th Gurkha Rifles in Quetta. In 1935 he survived the major earthquake that hit that city. The battalion moved to Assam in the aftermath, where it remained until early 1939.

In 1939, Walker moved with his battalion across India to Razmak, on the Northwest Frontier, where there had been turmoil since 1936. He distinguished himself and was recommended for the Military Cross.

In 1942, Walker was appointed General Staff Officer Grade 3 (GSO 3) on the staff of General Slim's Burma Corps, joining them near the oilfields at Yenangyaung in mid-April 1942. He remained with the

HQ as it walked back to India and was then appointed as an instructor at the Quetta staff college.

In early 1944, Walker was appointed second-in-command, alongside a new commanding officer, of the 4/8th Gurkha Rifles, who had suffered severely in the Arakan Campaign. In March the battalion was moved to the Imphal area, where the Japanese had launched a major offensive, and spent several months in hard fighting. In November he became the commanding officer, instigated a tough training regime and the battalion's motto, "Live Hard, Fight Hard, and when necessary Die Hard". Always a disciplinarian, he was a hard taskmaster and a totally professional soldier dedicated to hard training, and balanced by integrity, generosity, and warmth.

In early 1945 he led the 4/8th Gurkhas, part of IV Indian Corps, across the Irrawaddy River and hard fighting against the main body of the Japanese Army in Burma. In June he was appointed GSO 1 in his division's (7th Indian Division) Headquarters, although circumstances dictated that he had to return part time to 4/8th Gurkhas as their commanding officer again. This was a highly unusual situation. At the end of the war he was awarded the Distinguished Service Order and 7th Indian Infantry Division moved to occupy Thailand, where he was involved in negotiating the surrender of Japanese forces.

In 1948, the Emergency was declared in Malaya. Walker's immediate role was to train and equip the irregular Ferret Force. In late 1948, he was appointed Commandant of the Far East Training Centre in Johore Bahru with the task of training British units in jungle fighting. In 1950 he was appointed to command 1/6th Gurkha Rifles.

In 1954, he returned to UK as a senior staff officer in Headquarters Eastern Command where he was involved in planning and mounting the Suez operation in 1956.

In 1957, he was promoted to Brigadier and commander of 99th Gurkha Infantry Brigade in Malaya. This was the most demanding and important command in the Army, assigned the task of finally defeating the most formidable remaining terrorists in Johore – Operation Tiger. A feature was Walker's excellent relationship with Police Special Branch, painstaking development of intelligence, sustained ambushing, and his genius for training and inspiring confidence and enthusiasm.

In 1959, 99th Brigade was sent to Singapore for the forthcoming elections. Walker was told to take charge of internal security throughout Singapore. The problem was that 99th Brigade were highly skilled jungle fighters, while urban Singapore was a foreign land and internal security entirely new. Walker immediately instituted a typically thorough training program, which included writing the manual on the subject. *Internal Security in a City* became the army standard on the subject. In 1961, he was promoted General Officer Commanding 17th Gurkha Division and Major General, Brigade of Gurkhas.

Rumours about the axing of the Gurkhas emerged, and Walker played an astute hand, involving the King of Nepal and the US Ambassador there to protect them. It did not endear him to the Chief of the Imperial General Staff, and he came close to being sacked. However, on 8 December 1962, while he was in Nepal and some days walk from transport, a revolt broke out in Brunei. He reached Singapore 9 days later.

General Walker was appointed COMBRITBOR on 19 December with command over all British forces (land, sea, and air) in the colonies of Sarawak and North Borneo, and the protectorate of Brunei. The revolt was quickly mopped up, and incipient revolts in Sarawak were prevented by an influx of British and Gurkha troops. However, rumours of Indonesian sympathy for the insurgents and emerging hostility caused him concern. The situation gradually evolved into confrontation. However, Walker was master of the situation and developed an effective operational concept and tactics to contain the threat and most importantly retain the military initiative. The outcome was a successful campaign ending in August 1966.

He returned to the UK and was posted to NATO as Deputy Chief of Staff in charge of Plans, Operations, and Intelligence, H.Q., Allied Forces Central Europe headquarters in Paris, where his job was to plan and execute the headquarters move out of France. He accomplished this complex task on time and very efficiently. Promoted and knighted, he was appointed General Officer Commanding in Chief of Northern Command in the UK. Finally, in 1969, he was promoted to full General and appointed NATO's Commander in Chief Allied Forces Northern Europe with headquarters in Oslo. Walker saw his role as publicizing the threat. The region faced an overwhelming and expanding Soviet force, and while he did not expect Soviet direct attack, he did see a strategic threat of expanding influence aimed at neutralizing the Nordic countries (and possibly beyond) and clearing the path into the North Atlantic. Pointing this out did not endear him to some politicians and even his NATO superior. He retired from the army in 1972.

Walker began giving television interviews and took part in a documentary named *A Day in the Life of a General* which was never aired due to security reasons, although Walker believed it was banned because he was "revealing the true state of affairs which the politicians are hiding from the public."

By 1974, Walker had grown "shocked" by the state of the country in general and the "militancy" of the trade unions in particular. In July of that year he wrote a letter to *The Daily Telegraph* calling for "dynamic, invigorating, uplifting leadership … above party politics" which would "save" the country from "the Communist Trojan horse in our midst."

Shortly after this letter, the *London Evening News* gave Walker a front-page interview and asked him if he could imagine a situation in which the army could take over Britain. Walker responded: "Perhaps the country might choose rule by the gun in preference to anarchy." Even so, Walker always argued he hated the idea of a military government in Britain.

Thus, the General formed Civil Assistance which he claimed would supply volunteers in the event of a general strike. He boasted it had at least 100,000 members, which led Defence Secretary Roy Mason to interrupt his holiday by condemning this "near fascist groundswell".

Convinced by my meeting with the General, I enthusiastically assisted Brigadier Graham in establishing Civil Assistance in Norfolk. Over the next few months, considerable progress was made, and by mid-1974 we had over fifty local leaders throughout the county and felt strong enough to invite General Walker to visit us. In June a great meeting was held in Norwich Assembly House attended by some 200 members. Afterwards it was my privilege to entertain the General and his wife for dinner and overnight. I decided to invite leading members of the area who might not otherwise have encountered our principal guest. I think it fair to say that all were charmed by Walker, but few were convinced by his strong opinions. Out of politeness they nodded their heads, but they went away sceptical. As one was heard to comment, it was "just another of Michael's enthusiasms"!

On February 25 1975, all the county coordinators of Civil Assistance and their deputies were summoned to attend a meeting held at St Lawrence Jewry in the City of London. About 100 attended. General Walker made a rousing speech calling the British Left a "cancer", organizers of political strikes "traitors", and Labour MPs "subversives". He said that Civil Assistance would "act" against these in conjunction with the chief constables who in the main supported the organization.

Next day the *Morning Star*, the leading Communist newspaper, gave headlines to the meeting and listed the County Coordinators and their deputies in bold print as serious enemies of the Soviet Union. As a result of this, the Foreign Office warned me never to visit Russia! And, of course, I did not do so until the Soviet system was overthrown for good in 1991.

The final Norfolk gathering of Civil Assistance was held on 28 August that year (1975) when the Eastern Daily Press reported:

> Over 100 people attended a meeting of Civil Assistance at Binham Village Hall. Guest speaker was regional organizer, Major General H.E. Bredin.[71] and county organizer, Brigadier C.C. Graham talked about the movement and about the danger of communism. Mr Michael Wynne-Parker, deputy county coordinator, talked about the infiltration of communism into the Church, education and local politics.[72]

It was the last meeting because Margaret Thatcher was now at the helm, and Civil Assistance gradually faded away as the unions had met their match. England was saved from the communist threat, and Russia was delivered from tyranny.

---

71 Major-General Humphrey Edgar Nicholson Bredin (1916–2005) was a British soldier whose military service took him from 1930s Palestine via Dunkirk, North Africa and Italy to the Cold War in Germany.
72 *Eastern Daily Press*, 29 August 1975

10: Ralph Hammond-Innes

Ralph Hammond-Innes, CBE

Ralph had no children other than his thirty-five published books written in so many years.

I first met him at Ickworth, Suffolk's grand Palladian mansion home of the Hervey's – Earls and Marquesses of Bristol.[73] Late every December, Victor, the sixth Marquess, hosted a great pre-Christmas party, not to be missed even by those of us living in neighbouring Norfolk. In those remote rural areas of East Anglia, one thought nothing of driving fifty miles for a good party.

Victor, essentially a shy person, was nevertheless a thoughtful host who made every effort to make appropriate introductions. Whether his introducing me to Ralph was appropriate or not, it was most certainly to my advantage, as the years ahead came to prove.

Winking his right eye, he said to me, "You are a scribbler – meet a proper writer!"

My scribbling so far had been confined to my editorials of the Monarchist magazine, put together half-yearly and rather amateurishly by Victor, Jeffrey Fineston.[74] and myself. Of course, I had heard of Ralph, though, as I admitted in that first conversation over Victor's excellent vintage champagne, I had not read any of his (in those days) very well-known novels.

At that time I did not read novels – that is to say, modern novels. I suppose I was a literary snob. I felt I *should* read (and try to understand) Tolstoy, Dostoevsky, Dickens, Bronte, and Trollope; but I really thought nonfiction works were more interesting.

---

73 See chapter 7
74 Jeffrey Fineston – royal and society photographer and chronicler.

And popular fiction ... well ...?

Ralph was a true gentleman, concealing any egocentricity behind an appearance of genuine interest in those he met who, in turn, were put instantly at ease.

Boldly I asked him for his telephone number, and it wasn't long before I invited him and Dorothy, his wife, to dinner in Norfolk. He accepted. I was extremely happy. If I had had one ambition as a child, it was to be a writer. My aim in life was to meet published authors, and now I was about to receive and entertain one of Britain's most famous novelists.

Much thought went into that dinner. Most of my Norfolk neighbours were hunting, shooting, and fishing friends, though there were a few artists, naturalist artists of course, including J.C. Harrison,[75] Richard Robjent,[76] and Shirley Deterding.[77] The only one available was Shirley, and she, with Jimmy her husband, arrived in good time to help set the scene.

A car "screeched" up the drive, and I looked through the library windows to see the great man emerge. He was a man of immaculate appearance and meticulous manner, and I watched with interest as I saw him quickly change from his comfortable cardigan into his dinner jacket.

Though of gentle manner and quiet disposition, Ralph spoke with clarity and intensity, never wasting a word and leaving his listeners spellbound. From his arrival, through pre-dinner drinks, sitting at the table, and thereafter into the early hours, that great master of storytelling regaled us lucky few with his adventures in the far-flung places that were the basis of his novels.

As I came to appreciate later, Ralph's success as a novelist was based on his ability to relate real-life experiences within the context of an imaginative adventure story. He was primarily an *observer* of life. These powers of observation had been developed when Ralph was employed as a journalist at the *Financial Times*.

---

75 John Cyril Harrison (1898-1985) an artist, painted birds, animals, and landscapes.
76 Richard Robjent (born 1937) an artist, publisher, sportsman, and naturalist.
77 Shirley Carnt (Deterding) an artist and accomplished sportswoman.

English literature had been his favourite subject at school in Sussex, and journalism seemed an appropriate profession in those uncertain pre-war years. His first novel (*The Doppelganger*, 1937) marks the beginning of his prolific output, which developed despite his military activities in the Royal Artillery, where he rose to the rank of major, and his domestic preoccupations, most importantly his marriage to Dorothy[78] at the beginning of the war.

It was my greatest luck and happiness to get to know Ralph and Dorothy well over the next thirty years – indeed, until they died. They were a remarkable couple. With no children to distract them, they were completely devoted to each other in an undemanding and entirely civilized way. Each respected the other's "space". Neither tried to change the other. Each complimented the other in telepathic thought, word, and gracious deed. I have rarely met such a relationship in marriage.

Ralph and Dorothy had several shared passions (the secret of their long-lived happiness). Their central interest was the magical garden that they had created at Ayers End, Kersley, Suffolk. It was a traditional English garden where old scented roses mingled with herbaceous flowers, adjoining an abundant kitchen garden of vegetables, spice beds and fruit trees the whole surrounded by that essential perfectly mown lawn.

Their pre-dinner receptions, beginning in Ralph's Tudor library, always spilled out into this heavenly garden where champagne, mingled with the heavy dews of early evening, created an ethereal and intoxicating atmosphere. There, even a humble scribbler might imagine himself capable of becoming a writer!

Apart from a few neighbours and special friends, most of those privileged to sit at Ralph's table were of the meritocracy. Regulars included Christina Foyle,[79] founder of the famous bookshop and literary luncheons, and Baron Rolf Beck, inventor of Molyslip, a dry grease that is still used in car engines across the world today.

There was an aura of mystery around Rolf Beck, who resided at Layham Hall not far away from the Hammond-Innes' house. When

---

78 Dorothy Mary Lange (1911–1989) was an actress, writer and gardener.
79 Christina Agnes Lilian Foyle (1911– 1999) was an English bookseller and owner of Foyle's bookshop.

Ralph and Dorothy first knew him, his household included a partially domesticated bear that caused rather a stir in rural Suffolk. Rumour had it that Beck's father had been barber to Emperor Wilhelm. Upon his abdication, the Emperor, leaving Berlin by train, heard a voice calling from the platform, "Your Majesty! Your Majesty! I have not been paid!" Leaning out of the window of the departing train, the Emperor replied, "I have no money to give you, but I create you Baron Beck."

Whatever the truth, the Beck's appeared to have prospered, and it was generally accepted that Rolf Beck was a millionaire.

One night after a good dinner and in the absence of the ladies, one guest boldly asked the Baron to reveal how rich he was. Quickly taking out of his pocket a bulging wallet, Rolf produced some fifty bank cards. He explained how he drew a certain amount from the first card, paying it off with the second card, and so on, thus producing an enormous monthly cash flow. The secret, he explained, was simply earning enough to pay the monthly interest, about ten per cent of the whole. This was in 1978 when not so many people had bank (credit) cards – and certainly not fifty! He held us all spellbound by this financial wizardry and went on successfully for several more years to tell the tale.

Sailing and travelling were Ralph and Dorothy's other shared passions. As previously stated, Ralph's successful novels were based on real-life adventure and experience. Every early spring they would set off to explore a new part of the world, sometimes sailing or using long-distance trains, if not by air. During these trips, taking notes and many photographs, Ralph's imagination would be stimulated, and the plot of a new novel would emerge.

Arriving back at Kersley, he would exercise his keenly developed discipline within an established daily routine – an early breakfast, a walk round the garden, into his study from 8 a.m. until 1 p.m. (not to be disturbed), a light luncheon, a further walk and an hour's siesta, then back to the study to deal with the day's telephone calls (taken initially by his secretary), considerable fan mail, and diary planning.

Promptly at 6 p.m. this disciplined day would end. Then he would go into the garden for an hour before preparing for dinner and a bottle of champagne. Sometimes this would be with those favoured guests, in which case black tie would be worn, on other occasions, he would go out to dinner with friends and admirers, of which there were very many.

By autumn the book of the year would be written and it would usually be published in time for the Christmas market. During the winter Ralph would embark on a month's promotional visits to various parts of the United Kingdom (and sometimes beyond), signing endless copies of his latest work.

Dorothy was also a writer of considerable skill. She wrote beautifully produced volumes about the garden and their travels. Her books did not become internationally famous like Ralph's, but they are greatly valued by devotees of gardening and exotic foreign places.

Ralph became a true and consistent friend, always ready to give well thought out advice.

In 1989 I wrote my first book[80] and had grave doubts about whether I would sell even one copy! I mentioned this to Ralph who asked me to mail him the finished text, which I rather hesitatingly did. I will never forget that Saturday morning when the telephone rang and Ralph proclaimed it to be an interesting and readable work and announced that he had penned an introduction! What encouragement! To have England's most famous novelist write, "A compulsive and fascinating talker, it is only now, after all the years I have known him, that I have discovered he is also a good writer …"

Though Ralph's endorsement the book sold well, and this kindness was never forgotten. Encouragement costs little to give, but it can make all the difference to the course of the recipient's life.

---

80 *Bridge Over Troubled Water*, first edition in 1989.

11: Sergei Rodzianko

"*Sir the Bolsheviks are here.* They have come to kill you. Please leave at once!"

Sergei Rodzianko was in the first-floor drawing room of his Saint Petersburg house enjoying a few moments of tranquillity with his heavily pregnant wife when his gardener burst in.

"Take off your smock, Ruslan," replied Sergei and, realizing he had only minutes before the enemy would arrive, threw off his silk dressing gown and, donning the peasant's garb, kissed his wife and jumped out of the window.

He jumped into an entirely different world. His quick thinking and disguise had saved his life, but for what? As he escaped from a now alien Russia, leaving his home and (at least for many years) his family, only unknown territory lay ahead.

Well, it was not entirely unknown, for before the Soviet horror had been unleashed on an unsuspecting Russia, Sergei had travelled several times into Western Europe. There he had made friends. It was to those friends that he now turned.

Sergei hailed from a remarkable family steeped in the history of Russia. They were Cossacks – not just Cossacks but *starshyna*, men of authority and leadership for over four hundred years. Their origins were in the Poltava and Novomoskovsk regions in what is now Ukraine where they maintained vast estates and official positions.

The strength of Tsarist Russia was its ability to include and absorb a multiplicity of regional notables of every race and religion. Catherine the Great and Prince Potemkin had set in motion this system, whereby "western" pragmatism (for example, the Baltic Barons who administered the Russian Empire) combined with "eastern" inspiration to create a balance of regional aspiration with a sense of belonging. The Empire was a family and the Tsar, "Little Father", its protector.

From earliest times the forebears of the Cossacks, who dwelt around the river Don, played their often dramatic role in Russia's history. So it was not unusual that the Rodziankos should rise, prosper, and play an important part in the affairs of the Empire.

Their role was political and military. Sergei's uncle Michael had risen to become president of the controversial Duma. Sergei himself, following in the footsteps of his father, General Paul Rodzianko, and elder brother, also Paul, was a soldier.

Ever admiring his brother, Sergei had dreamed of becoming a soldier, and at the earliest possible moment he entered the *Corp de Pages* until he was old enough to join the family regiment, the Chevalier Guards. Under his brother Paul's guiding hand and with his not inconsiderable influence, by the age of eighteen Sergei joined his compatriots on the Polish front.

Initially these were exciting and thrilling times. Confidence was high, and Russia was yet to suffer the horrendous casualties inflicted by the well-organized German forces. The sheer size of the front, the lamentable lack of ammunition, and ultimately the mismanagement of the railways through the corruption of many officials, were yet to cast the shadow of defeat that ultimately led to the destruction of Imperial Russia and the terrifying imposition of ruthless communism.

Sergei was safely back (as he thought) in Petersburg and happily married to his young and lovely wife when the real horror struck.

Little is known of Sergei's progress following his dramatic escape, and when I got to know him he was eighty and his memory was a little vague.

What struck one at that first meeting was his enthusiasm. The years had not wearied him nor the sufferings of his early years embittered him; he was at ease with himself and the whole world.

Princess Valentine Galitzine had introduced us, and as he sat at the table and after a couple of healthy vodkas, he related what he wanted to relate – maybe a little embellished with time, but none the worse for that.

The Cossacks are first and foremost horsemen. Horses are their life, and they know how to ride. His early training in horsemanship was to be of huge benefit to Sergei throughout his unexpected exile.

According to Prince Sergei Obolensky,[81] whom I met in New York at the Waldorf Astoria Hotel in 1967 where I witnessed his performance of the famous dagger dance, Sergei first found his way to Switzerland where he played in championship tennis tournaments, though he mentioned nothing of this to me. Rather, he stressed his early participation in continental horse shows.

From Switzerland he went, somehow, to Canada where he trained horses on a ranch.

But it was to England and his earliest memories there that Sergei mostly referred in his twilight years. Englishmen and Cossacks are tied together by their passionate devotion to horses, and thus Sergei found and relished his second home.

And where in England should he inevitably be drawn but to Leicestershire, the heartland of hunting, and it was there that he almost implanted his Russian roots.

Englishmen *think* they know how to ride. Cossacks *really* know how to ride! So with some diplomacy and aided by perceptive friends, Sergei began to share his equestrian secrets. First training horses for various people, he inevitably advanced to training the riders, first without saddle and later without stirrups or reins. When a rider was able to jump his horse over a car without saddle, stirrups, or reins he was on his way to becoming a full-blooded Cossack!

Things did not always go smoothly, however. Paul Rodzianko relates:

> Although a beautiful rider he was rather cowed by the English hunting women who cursed him at gates and told him to "shut up, we're hunting" if he spoke when hounds ran.[82]

Now familiar in English hunting country, Sergei was also becoming famous in the European show-jumping world and appeared regularly at horse shows in Germany, France, and Austria.

---

81 Prince Sergei (Serge) Obolensky (1890–1978) author of *One Man in His Time – The Memoirs of Sergei Obolensky*, published in 1958.

82 *Tattered Banners* (personal biography) by Paul Rodzianko. Paul had famously rescued Joy, Tsarevich Alexei's spaniel in Yekaterinburg after the Imperial families' murder.

Relates Paul:

Sergei had a horse, Rosalynd, which he trained to jump without reins. At Vienna Horse Show he gave an exhibition but unfortunately on this occasion Rosalynd did not stop. Having jumped the course once, she went on around and around while poor Sergei "whoa-ed" in vain and his friends roared with laughter.[83]

As I have said, Sergei was about eighty when I met him in London, and by this time he had become an established portrait painter. A few years previously he had taken quite a hard fall whilst out hunting. About this time an old Russian friend had put it about that Sergei had a secret talent for drawing. His friend had witnessed instant sketches appear during idle moments in the trenches – sketches of comrades, some just about to die, whose hastily sketched portraits would bring comfort to several widows and orphans. The rumour of Sergei's talent spread amongst his hunting friends, who spontaneously agreed to put together enough money to allow him to perfect his art under the professional tutorage of Oskar Kokoschka.[84]

Many of the families of Sergei's hunting and racing friends began to invite him to their country houses, this time not to teach them how to ride or to train their horses but to paint their portraits and portraits of their children, ponies, and dogs.

Over dinner Sergei would regale his hosts with stories of old Russia. His favourite, especially in the presence of children, were stories of Mishka the family bear.

Mishka was the survivor of a hunting adventure in 1908 and had been brought up as a pet in the Rodzianko household. He became one of the family and would walk about, often on his hind feet which made him as tall as Sergei!

One day Mishka wandered off into the local village and entered a beer store where he helped himself to an open bottle. The terrified

---

83 *Tattered Banners,* Paul Rodzianko
84 Oskar Kokoschka (1866–1980) was an Austrian artist, poet, and playwright best known for his intense expressionistic portraits and landscapes.

owner stood by helplessly while Mishka downed the pint of beer before ambling off back home. Enjoying this experience, Mishka made it a daily afternoon excursion. Somewhat to Sergei's father's surprise, he began to receive a weekly bill for Mishka's daily beer!

One day after returning home, Mishka, rather tired after his excursion, sat down to rest in the courtyard. Out came the cook to throw corn to the chickens. As soon as she departed, Mishka scooped up some gravel in his large paw and, mimicking the cook, threw it towards the chickens which unsuspectingly ran forward to him. Thus Mishka found the way to enjoy a chicken lunch after an invigorating beer.

In 1973, Sergei said he would like to paint my portrait, the first version of which would be in pastel. During the second sitting he announced that he was to attend a Russian ball but that he had lost his dinner jacket. I suspected that it was really so old that it had fallen to pieces. I had also decided to attend the same ball, but luckily I had two jackets – an old one and one just recently made. The latter I lent to Sergei.

How he enjoyed that evening – dancing almost every dance until the early hours. We shared a taxi, and I dropped him off in Chesterfield Street on my way home.

"Good night, Michael, see you next week for your next sitting," said my friend. But it was not to be. Two days later, Prince George Galitzine,[85] who turned out to be Sergei's trustee, telephoned me to inform me that our friend had died in his sleep.

"What was he wearing?" I asked

"A splendid dinner jacket!"

Sergei had returned home, gone to bed with happy dreams of the ball, and died. He had left me a book, three photographs of his show-jumping exploits, a sketch by Oskar Kokoschka, and my unfinished portrait, forever a cherished reminder of this remarkable man.

What a life! Born into one of Russia's richest and most influential families, Sergei died in a one-bedroom rented flat, a poor artist in London.

Maybe to lose everything is to find oneself?

---

85 Major Prince George Galitzine (1916–1992)

12: Said Hammami

*B*efore the Six-Day War *of* 1967, as a young man I had no strong feelings about the Palestine issue. I had met a few Jewish people who also appeared to care little about events in the Holy Land. I knew no Arabs.

My experience of that short war and later visits to Palestinian refugee camps changed all that. I felt that everything should be done to alert the world's attention to the shocking Israeli occupation of the Arabs' native land.

In December 1973, Ahmed Khalil, a Palestinian lawyer, was quoted in a British newspaper:[86]

> I was born in Haifa (Palestine) and so were my father and my grandfather. Now I am a refugee. Golda Meir[87] was born in Russia, educated in America and now she is prime minister of my country! I studied law with Abba Eban[88] at Cambridge. He was born in South Africa and educated in England. Now he lives in my country and I can't.

The basis of the new state of Israel[89] was the removal of one people from their native land in order to supplant them with another.

---

86 *The Guardian*, 22 December 1973.
87 Golda Meir, born Golda Mabovitch (1898–1978), was the fourth prime minister of the State of Israel 1969–74.
88 Abba Eban, born Aubrey Solomon Meir Eban (1915–2002) was an Israeli diplomat and politician.
89 Established in 1948.

In the same year that Ahmed Khalil wrote his piece in *The Guardian*, Said Hammami was appointed by Yasser Arafat[90] to be the first diplomatic delegate of the PLO[91] to the United Kingdom, heading their office in London.

Born in Jaffa in 1941, Said Hammami fled the British Mandate of Palestine with his family upon the breakout of hostilities which preceded the creation of the State of Israel. After a brief stop in Egypt, they moved to Lebanon and then settled in Jordan, where Hammami attended high school. From there he went on to university in Syria to study English literature. It was in Damascus that his interest in politics began. For a short time he became a school teacher in Saudi Arabia, but soon his devotion to the Palestinian cause took him back to Syria, where he became an enthusiastic founder member of the PLO in 1964. He quickly climbed the ranks of the organization and became a member of the Palestine National Council. It was the great impression that he had made on Arafat that led to his arrival in London.

I had become chairman of the East Region of the Council for Arab-British Understanding in 1970 at the young age of twenty-five. This was due to the sponsorship of three leading Arabists. I met my local MP Ian Gilmour[92] after he had read my articles about the Six-Day War. He in turn introduced me to Lord Caradon,[93] who became a good and encouraging friend and introduced me to John Reddaway,[94] who was at the time leading CAABU nationally.

In 1974, John Reddaway introduced me to Said Hammami at the Travellers' Club in Pall Mall over lunch. One could not help liking Said instantly. He was of a quiet, calm disposition with a sharp intellect

---

90 Mohammed Yasser Abdel Rahman Abdel Raouf Arafat al-Qudwa al-Husseini (1929–2004), popularly known as Yasser Arafat, Palestinian Leader and a Laureate of the Nobel Prize.
91 The Palestine Liberation Organization (PLO) is a political and paramilitary organization founded in 1964.
92 Ian Hedworth John Little Gilmour, Baron Gilmour of Craigmillar (1926–2007) was a Conservative politician in the United Kingdom.
93 Hugh Mackintosh Foot, Baron Caradon (1907–90), was a British colonial administrator and diplomat who oversaw moves to independence in various colonies and was UK representative to the United Nations.
94 John Reddaway (1916–90) was a diplomat who served as Deputy Commissioner-General of the United Nations Relief and Works Agency, 1960-8.

and a natural diplomatic manner. He was no fanatic and argued the Palestinian case in a balanced and logical manner. He was the very best possible advocate of the cause.

He had already begun to promote co-existence between the Palestinians and Israelis, calling for a two-state solution even in those far-off days. (We have made little progress since!) Thus, he was a moderate and not a trigger-happy revolutionary. The Zionist media had long put it about that the PLO was a terrorist organization, and many people are ultimately influenced by the media.

In London Said was busy establishing contact with British politicians and journalists and, rather controversially from the Arab point of view, building up relations with Israeli peace activists, most notably Uri Avnery.[95]

At the end of luncheon I suggested to Said Hammami that it was vital that he take his message out of London into the provinces, where people were in total ignorance of the Palestinians' real plight. He and John Reddaway agreed with this and challenged me to do something about it.

I decided to hold a reception in Norwich at which Said Hammami would be guest of honour. To add credibility, I asked Dick Gurney,[96] then local Director of Barclays Bank, to sponsor the event and host it at the bank's headquarters in Norwich. Without hesitation he agreed – a courageous man.

The date was set for 3rd October 1975 and invitations went out. Disappointingly, the initial response was slow. The rumour was about that the head of a terrorist organization was about to arrive and would be best avoided! It took many hours of telephone calls to counter these malicious rumours, and the more courageous invitees began to accept.

As it turned out, the event was a great success. Several significant Arab diplomats, including the head of the Arab Diplomatic Corps, Lakhdar Brahimi the Algerian ambassador, accompanied Said Hammami. Local dignitaries, political, civic, and social, turned up and there was widespread media coverage. This was the first time the

---

95 Uri Avnery (born 1923) an Israeli writer and founder of the Gush Shalom peace movement.
96 Richard Quintin Gurney (1914–1980)

Arab Diplomatic Corps had travelled into the provinces, and it set an important precedent for the future.

Said Hammami spoke eloquently, and for the first time many present began to understand the Palestinian point of view.

"Not a bad chap," said one local grandee, "but where was his gun? Rather disappointing!"

I kept in close touch with Said and his wife over the next three years, during which time he was having an increasingly positive impact on London and political life.

On January 4 1978 came the shocking news. Said had been gunned down in his office in Green street, Mayfair. Ironically, his assassination had been organized by *Palestinian* hardliners who were unable to contemplate any two-state solution, led by Sabri al Banna, otherwise known as Abu Nidal[97] (probably the *real* Lockerbie Pan Am[98] murderer).

It was Said's *Israeli* friend who was to write his biography entitled *My Friend the Enemy*.

A few years later, I lunched in a Lebanese restaurant, Al Basha, in Kensington High Street, London. Asking for the bill, I was surprised to receive the response, "No bill for you, Sir! I know what you did for Said. He was my cousin, and you are now family."

---

97 Abu Nidal, born Sabri Khalil al-Banna (1937–2002), was the founder of Fatah – The Revolutionary Council (also known as the Abu Nidal Organization (ANO)).
98 Pan American World Airways, commonly known as Pan Am, was the principal United States international air carrier from the late 1920s until its collapse on December 4 1991.

13: Jonathan Guinness

Jonathan Bryan Guinness, 3rd Baron Moyne

Jonathan has the piercing blue Mitford eyes inherited from his mother, Diana Mosley.[99] Diana had divorced Jonathan's father[100] and finally married Sir Oswald Mosley,[101] and Adolph Hitler[102] had been the best man.

"What beautiful eyes you have, Lady Mosley," said the Fuhrer.

"What lovely hair you have," was her reply.

Jonathan and his by now most distinguished brother Desmond[103] had an unusual but not unhappy childhood. Jonathan remembers visiting his mother and stepfather in Holloway Prison during holidays from Eton. Churchill had decided that Mosley was too dangerous to be on the loose during World War II. In fact, Mosley used the time in prison wisely; he engaged in rigorous daily exercise and devoured every book he could get hold of. Soon the Mosleys were allowed to share quarters and developed a not uncomfortable lifestyle! Jonathan, though not entirely endorsing his political philosophy, came to admire his notorious stepfather.

---

99 Diana Mitford, Lady Mosley, née Freeman-Mitford (1910–2003), was one of Britain's noted Mitford sisters.

100 Bryan Walter Guinness, 2nd Baron Moyne (1905–1992), was an heir to part of the Guinness family brewing fortune, lawyer, poet, and novelist.

101 Sir Oswald Ernald Mosley, 6th Baronet (1896–1980), was a British politician, known principally as the founder of the British Union of Fascists.

102 Adolf Hitler (1889–1945) was an Austrian-born German politician and the leader of the National Socialist German Workers Party, commonly known as the Nazi Party.

103 Hon. Desmond Guinness (born 1931) an Irish author on Georgian art and architecture and a conservationist, founder and chairman of the Irish Georgian Society.

But I think it is the Mitford qualities that have most influenced his life and work – sparkling wit, empathetic skill, analytical memory, high intelligence, and charm.

Jonathan is a civilized man. We first met at a dinner in Dartmouth House in 1975. The conversation ranged from domestic political issues to international affairs, and I remember his forthright comments, at times controversial, but so eloquently put that they went largely undisputed.

He invited me to join the *Monday Club*[104] of which he was chairman at the time. At that time the club was a significant debating society within the Conservative Party, and I attended several interesting events.

It was at one of those events that I had a long conversation with Jonathan, who revealed that, despite the Guinness Family fortune, his own financial position was precarious. Further meetings led us both to the conclusion that our mutual eminent connections could be useful to aspiring businessmen and thus Introcom (International) Ltd was born.

Over the next few years and with the additional help of Sir William Shelton[105] and Sir Charles Blois,[106] several projects were embarked upon – some with more success than others – and though we were not highly successful in financial terms, we had plenty of adventures. Perhaps truly worthy of *The Guinness Book of Records*[107] was our achievement in flying the first jumbo jet (Boeing 747) into Central Asia.

Little could have prepared him for the international headlines that appeared almost daily in the *Financial Times*[108] concerning the Trustor Affair. Known as the greatest financial fraud in Swedish history,[109] the

---

104 The Conservative Monday Club (widely known as the Monday Club) is a British pressure group "on the right wing" of the Conservative Party, founded in the early 1960s.
105 Sir William Jeremy Masefield Shelton, commonly known as Bill Shelton (1929–2003) was a Conservative Party politician in the United Kingdom.
106 Sir Charles Nicholas Gervase Blois, 11th Baronet (born 1939)
107 *Guinness World Records*, known until 2000 as *The Guinness Book of Records* is a reference book published annually, containing a collection of world records, both human achievements and the extremes of the natural world.
108 From December 1997 thought 1998.
109 Gunnar Lindstedt author of many articles and a book about Trustor first broke the scandal in the Swedish press on 31 October 1997.

Trustor Affair would have taxed the genius of Sherlock Holmes and been worthy of the brain of Moriarty,[110] Still unsolved to this day, the essence was as follows.

Joachim Posner, alias Joe Falk – the Moriarty of the case – dreamed up the fraud whilst in prison in Denmark for a similar but far smaller crime. Whilst there, he brought his cousin Thomas Jisander into the plot, who in turn recruited the then rather naive and innocent Peter Mattson.[111] His job was to find an appropriate name – someone of rank and perceived wealth whose position as head of a business empire would not be questioned – and what better name than Guinness?

In 1996, Peter approached Jonathan, whom he had met much earlier as a client of Introcom, explaining that there was an opportunity for him to be elected chairman of Trustor at the next AGM in Stockholm.[112] The reason given was that Trustor, now an international business, would be moving its HQ to London. The post would bring a generous remuneration, share options, an expense allowance, and all the future security Jonathan could need – an offer he could hardly refuse!

To all intents and purposes Trustor was a highly successful and respectable company, and the removal of its HQ to London had certain logic. There is no question that Jonathan perceived this to be a perfectly legitimate situation that he was very fortunate to be involved in. Very quickly he learned Swedish (he is an accomplished linguist) and, as predicted, found himself elected chairman and occupying a splendid office suit in London's prestigious Berkeley Square.

What happened over the next few months is extremely well documented not only in the press but in several books, films, and TV documentaries. Suffice it to say that £50 million spread quickly through a multiplicity of bank accounts until it evaporated, apparently into thin air.[113]

To his shock and horror and (as it became clear) most unjustly, Jonathan was arrested together with the other main players. Only

---

110 Professor James Moriarty is a fictional character and the archenemy of the detective Sherlock Holmes in the fiction of Sir Arthur Conan Doyle.
111 Peter Mattsson – Swedish businessman.
112 Trustor was already a leading company in the Stockholm exchange.
113 Even so, the public shareholders had little appetite for a prosecution as despite the disappearance of the £50 million, the shares had actually risen in value.

Posner escaped arrest; he simply disappeared, only to reappear from time to time (a veritable Scarlet Pimpernel[114] but without honour) to tempt the extremely frustrated Swedish authorities. To this day he has not been brought to justice.

A very long trial ensued. I visited Jonathan in Stockholm and found him philosophical, despite facing a probable four-year prison sentence.

"I will spend the time in peace and quiet at the expense of the state and be able to concentrate on writing," he said. "There is a television, and visitors are allowed weekly." He was resigned to his fate.

Eileen Hillam had been recruited by Trustor to act as a PA. Attractive, highly intelligent, and articulate, she was entirely suited to this somewhat chaotic role. As Introcom, via Jonathan's good offices, had been appointed PR consultant[115] to the company I saw a good deal of Eileen and we became friends.

It was not unnatural, therefore, that well into Jonathan's trial I would invite Eileen to Sunday morning drinks at my Kensington apartment. As she drank her second glass of champagne, she opened her handbag (that secret weapon of every woman) and produced a rather tattered cheque.

"Why, Eileen, this is a Trustor cheque four years old!"

"Yes, I kept it as a memento. I was actually paid in cash."

I looked at the cheque more carefully. There was something wrong with the signature.

"This is not Jonathan's signature. I know it well," I said.

"You are right, he never signed. Others signed for him!"

At once the light dawned.

"Eileen you *must* take this cheque at once to Stockholm. It will prove Jonathan's innocence."

Eileen tried to snatch the cheque back.

"I cannot. *They* will kill me!"

I pocketed the cheque. Eileen ran out of the apartment, and I have not seen her since. Without delay I was on a flight to Stockholm

---

114 *The Scarlet Pimpernel* is a classic play and adventure novel by Baroness Emmuska Orczy, set during the Reign of Terror following the start of the French Revolution.

115 Her main task was to organize the Grand London Opening with Madonna and Margaret Thatcher leading the Guest List. Sadly it was not to take place!

just as the prosecution was winding up their case. Suffice it to say that the cheque provided the evidence that was required to get Jonathan acquitted, which happened the next day.

Is there, as Schweitzer[116] suggested, a significance in events? I believe there is.

---

116 Albert Schweitzer (1875–1965) was a Franco-German (Alsatian) theologian, organist, philosopher, and physician.

Images

Archimandrite Count Anthony Grabbe, Norwich, 1970.

Victor Hervey, 6th Marquess of Bristol, Savoy Hotel, 1973.

The author with General Sir John Glubb
(Glubb Pasha), Norwich, 1973.

Ralph Hammond-Innes, Count Nikolai Tolstoy and
the author, Bury St Edmunds, Suffolk, 1975.

Sergei Rodzianko jumping Rosalynd without reins, 1912.

Portrait of the author by Sergei Rodzianko, London, 1974.

Said Hammami at a reception in Norwich, 1975.

Lord Moyne (Jonathan Guinness) and the Hon Desmond Guinness, Kadriorg Palace, Estonia, 2007.

HRH Princess Katarina of Yugoslavia, Tallinn, 2005.

Lord Rix (Brian Rix), London, 1981.

The author with President J.R. Jayewardene, Major Anthony Gurney and Madam Jayewardene, Manor Farm, Northrepps, Norfolk, 1981.

An informal glimpse of President Jayewardene's private residence, Ward Place in Colombo. Also present are Mr Laksman Wijewardene, Dr Amerasinghe and the author, 1981.

President Premadasa of Sri Lanka with the author and Dr Nissanka Wijeyeratne, ESU Headquarters, Colombo, Sri Lanka, 1982

Sir Dai Llewellyn, 1993.

Margaret Thatcher signing her memoir *The Downing Street Years* for Saif Gaddafi, 2002.

Jim Davidson with Simon Gurney, HRH Princess Katarina and Jafar Ramini, Carlton Club, London, 1996.

General Shafik Jumean with Saif Gaddafi, London, 1999.

HRH Prince Muhammad of Jordan with General
Shafik Jumean, Amman, Jordan, 1999.

HRH Prince Andrew (Duke of York) with
Summer Watson, London, 2000.

Vera Protasova, London, 2002.

14: Katarina

HRH Princess Katarina of Yugoslavia

An early memory of Katarina is of a glorious summer's day in Norfolk that provided an opportunity for a game of croquet. First thing that morning, the plan had been to take an inaugural flight in a primitive-looking microlight glider – a sort of electric riding lawn mower with wings that had been invented by a neighbour. Katarina was keen on any adventure – the more dangerous the better – but luckily the neighbour had run out of fuel.

Though it may look innocent enough to the uninitiated, croquet is potentially dangerous, especially when one of the participants is Katarina, who can swing a croquet stick with ferocious accuracy and unexpected energy. Her polo skills are another matter!

The croquet game continued to gather momentum until most of the players had been knocked out – some almost literally. The two of us were left, but luckily there came the welcome call to tea. And those were the days of real English teas – scones loaded with fresh cream and homemade strawberry jam, teacakes, fruitcake – not to forget the thinly sliced cucumber sandwiches. The day wore on, and soon evening cocktails led to dinner, and dangers were over for the time being.

Katarina is truly a princess of Europe. A direct descendent of Queen Victoria, granddaughter of King Peter of Yugoslavia, granddaughter of Queen Marie of Rumania, she is closely related to all the royal families of Europe. She is a reminder of an older Europe when society moved effortlessly between Paris, St Petersburg, London, and Berlin.

From my earliest days I had been close to Katarina's father, Prince Tomislav. He had adapted to English country life rather well after the turmoil of his earlier days, but his heart always remained in Yugoslavia, and at the earliest opportunity, following Tito's death, he returned to Belgrade to the delight and encouragement of the local people with whom he was immensely popular.

Following her happy childhood days on her father's fruit farm in Kent, Katarina saw less and less of her father as he spent more time away, and thus she grew closer to her friends.

Despite being the "royalest of the royals",[117] she had to work hard to make her way in life (happy days at Harrods as a manager, for example), but this has stood her in very good stead, developing within her a realistic and practical streak which, together with that love of adventure and a fine sense of humour, makes her the popular and charismatic figure she is.

"The laughing princess" is what one journalist[118] called her, and it sums her up well. Hers is not the hollow laughter of sarcasm but the genuine laughter of someone who understands the humour of life and wishes to share her happiness with others.

Katarina is a natural communicator. When she was eighteen, she persuaded her father and me to take her to Annabel's. It was teeming with people that night, and no sooner had we entered than we lost Katarina in the crowd. Several glasses of champagne later, I found her surrounded by a group of men who appeared to be completely spellbound by her monologue. She was a fairly well-oiled princess surrounded by her first willing courtiers, and all were enjoying every moment of it.

As the years went by, Katarina began to be invited to become either president or patron of several organizations. One of the most important was the Inaugural Ball Committee of the British Forces Foundation. This organization was founded by Jim Davidson[119] to provide live entertainment to British troops stationed abroad, often in remote and desolate places. As a natural entertainer herself, perhaps Katarina was the very best choice for this particular role.

Unfortunately, just five days before the Inaugural Ball – whose guest list now included Margaret Thatcher and the Spice Girls – NATO, including British forces, made its attack on Yugoslavia (Serbia).

---

117 Nigel Dempster, *Daily Mail*
118 Paul Halloran – freelance investigative journalist.
119 See chapter 24

Diplomacy quickly came into play, and Katarina of Yugoslavia graciously but sadly withdrew.

Her other patronages have been rather more permanent. Most notable to date has been her presidency of the UK Guild of Travel and Tourism. In this role Katarina excels. She is an enthusiastic traveller and a popular speaker at Guild events in such august surroundings as the House of Lords.

As a European princess, it is appropriate that Katarina's patronage is not confined to the United Kingdom. In 2005 she became patron of the St George Foundation headquartered in Estonia. The foundation supports cultural and social projects within an Orthodox context. It is most significant, therefore, that an Orthodox royal should be patron. (It is not always realized that many European royals are, or at least were, Orthodox, including the Rumanians, Bulgarians, Greek, and Russian royal houses. Indeed, Prince Philip, consort of HM Queen Elizabeth, was born and baptized into the ancient faith.)

As patron of the St George Foundation, Katarina made her first visit to Estonia in October 2005. It was a strenuous and challenging couple of days, beginning at 3.30 a.m. when she was driven from her house in West Sussex to Luton airport.

Upon arrival in Tallinn at 12.30, she was whisked off to a welcoming luncheon aboard the *Admiral*, a restored St Petersburg vessel owned by a delightful Serbian couple who had known Katarina's father Prince Tomislav in the good old days. The host was the renowned Metropolitan Cornelius, head of the Russian Orthodox Church in Estonia and chairman of the foundation.

After a tour of Tallinn Old Town and a reception in the Town Hall hosted by Toomas Vitsut, chairman of Tallinn City Council, Katarina was able to return to the gracious surroundings of the Hotel Schlossle, but only for a few hours. At 6 a.m. breakfast was served before I joined her for a marathon tour of northeast Estonia. Setting off at high speed in a black Mercedes followed by security outriders, we first went to Rakvere, where we were greeted by the lovely sound of church bells. After paying homage at the shrine of Rakvere's famous martyr, St Sergy Florinsky, we hastened on to Puhtitsa Convent. Anyone who has been fortunate enough to visit this oasis of Russian spirituality and culture will never forget the first breath-taking sight of the Puhtitsa cupolas gleaming amidst the glorious woodland setting. It is natural to stop the car and pause to take in the inspiring view, and we did so despite the hectic schedule.

Abbess Varvara, most famous and beloved amongst Orthodox people, greeted Katarina and led us into a fabulous banquet, where we relaxed and enjoyed the convivial company before embarking onwards to Narva.

Once the social capital of the region, Narva was devastated during the Second World War. Little was left of the old city apart from its ancient Cathedral Church of the Resurrection. There we were welcomed by priest and people and the splendid choir which sang – perhaps for the first time since the revolution – "God save the Tsar". It was a moving moment. Father Nikolai Terentiev pointed out to Katarina that she was the first close member of the imperial family to visit the church since her ancestors, Alexander III and Kaiser Wilhelm II. It was remarkable to think of those two emperors, one Orthodox the other Protestant, together in that church.

Finally, there was another banquet given by the chairman of Narva Council, before we set off for the journey back to Tallinn.

It had been a long day during which Katarina had been presented with numerous bouquets. The car was like a flower shop, including many strongly scented lilies, which are a nightmare for any like myself who suffers from hay fever allergy.

What could we do with so many flowers but donate them, as we did, to an amazed group of elderly women who were talking together outside a rather rundown block of flats on the edge of town! Hopefully, their lives were a little cheered. We arrived back in Tallinn unencumbered except for the most beautiful bouquet of roses that had been presented to Katarina by Abbess Varvara and which accompanied her back to England.

It is not easy for a modern princess. Sadly, for many today monarchy is linked to the past, and history is a neglected subject with the consequent erosion of tradition. The Blairs and the Beckhams became the standard-bearers of the twenty-first century, but their day is already waning as their lives come under the constant scrutiny of the penetrative media, revealing that they leave neither an abiding legacy nor any inspiration.

The sense of duty accompanied by the joyous laughter of Katarina and her ilk may prevail after all.

15: Brian Rix

Brian Norman Roger Rix, Baron Rix, CBE

"*Always take off your socks* first or you end up looking like a Brian Rix farce."

Thus reported "Merkin on Paris" on 7 April 2010. He was commenting on a recent article written by Brian Rix in *The Guardian* newspaper[120] entitled "The Whitehall Farces had a major role in the TV-theatre relationship". And who could be more qualified to make such a claim than the "King of Farce" himself? For such an accolade had been awarded to Brian for as long as most of us can remember.

Whether dropping his trousers or taking off his socks, Brian has become a legend in his own lifetime in the realm of entertainment.

He is his own man, not fitting into any category and beyond objective definition. An actor, yes – but more. A comedian, yes – but more again. An "actor-manager" was one description used during his most famous Whitehall Theatre days, but then he became almost as well known on TV and in films as on the stage. One followed another during his heyday in the sixties and seventies.

When I read *The Guardian* article, my main thought was that I was glad my old friend was still alive and kicking at the ripe young age of 86!

Though our meeting on the London-Norwich express on June 5 1981, has become a noteworthy date covered in various newspapers, magazines, and books,[121] my first memory of Brian goes back to 1959. It was a special treat – a school outing to London's West End. The show

---

120 *The Guardian*, April 7 2010.
121 See, for example, *Farce about Face* by Brian Rix, Header and Stoughton, 1989; British Rail archives; *Financial Times* etc.

was *Dry Rot* at the Whitehall Theatre, and it was my first impression of the remarkable Brian Rix.

One did not then attend theatres often, and going to London was itself quite an event for a fourteen-year-old from the country. Bearing all this in mind, Brian nevertheless remained in my thoughts as a character of almost charismatic proportion, larger than life and above all "great fun". And that, very many years later, still summed him up in my estimation. On stage, his sense of humour, not created by learning some humorous lines written by others, poured out of his being, and later I was to learn it did so in real life also. And, may I add, despite the dropped trousers, his humour was never course or vulgar. In other words, it was fit for "ladies and gentlemen" and therefore always uplifting. He taught me the meaning of the *Reader's Digest*[122] motto "Laughter is the best medicine."

So, as someone once observed, "the impressions of childhood remain with us forever." Brian made a good and lasting impression.

Now to that fateful train journey. I had enjoyed a very late dinner and several hours at Annabel's, ending with breakfast at 4 a.m. Sleeping soundly, I missed the early train back home to Norfolk and ended up on the 11.30. Sinking into my seat, I realized that I had forgotten to get a copy of *The Times* at the station. To my amazement, a copy suddenly appeared before my very eyes – or at least the covers did. I knocked, somewhat timidly, on the front page which was lowered, revealing the face of a pretty young woman. Luckily, she did not seem to mind when I asked her if I might have the paper after she had finished with it. No sooner had this happened than a train inspector opened the carriage door and announced that a special reduced-price lunch was now being served. The young woman at once got up and without thought or hesitation I followed her straight into the restaurant car. She sat down and I, quickly scanning the dining car and seeing no other spare seats, had no alternative than to sit opposite her. I was, however, quickly put at ease when she said, "Oh, I am sorry; I forgot to give you the paper!"

Luncheon was served, and we struck up a conversation. She said she was leaving the train at Ipswich and asked me where I was headed

---

122 *Reader's Digest* is a monthly general-interest family magazine with circulation of 17 million.

for. I said Norwich. "Oh," she said, "my cousin lives there, Philippa Gurney.[123]" Philippa just happened to be my wife's cousin!

"Please, would you mind giving her my new address and telephone number?" said my new friend, and at once she scribbled down the information and handed it to me just as the train entered Ipswich station.

It was at this point that Brian entered my life.

I had already noticed his famous face as he was sitting at the opposite table. Now as the pretty girl left my table, I was emboldened to greet him and invited him to join in a further glass of wine (in Brian's version, it is coffee![124]).

He at once asked me "What secret charms did you use to ask a beautiful young woman, clearly a stranger, to give you her telephone number within such a short time?" He had seen the action but failed to hear the explanation. So reluctantly I had to admit that it was not my charm but a practical and unexpected family matter that had led to the handing over of her contact details!

After a few pleasantries, I asked Brian what was taking him to Norwich. He explained that he was to deliver a speech at the Institute of Health Service Administrators. I could think of nothing more boring and was just about to ask him why when he made a remarkable statement.

"You are familiar with St Paul's vision on the road to Damascus?"

"Yes, of course."

"It happened to me. I was on a train in the West Country when I read an advertisement. It was on behalf of Mencap[125] and offered the position of director general. I knew at once that it was intended for me."

Brian then went on to describe how he had applied for the post and been appointed. He had consequently given up the theatre and now rejoiced in the title Secretary-General of Mencap. Only those who remember his supremacy of the stage at that time can understand the sacrifice he made.

---

123 Now Lady Dannatt, wife of General Sir Richard Dannatt.
124 Brian Rix, *Farce about Face*, page 132.
125 The Royal Society for Mentally Handicapped Children and Adults.

"The problem," he said, "is money. We just don't have enough, and my present preoccupation is how to raise sufficient capital to permanently fund the charity."

By now we had reached Norwich. We had exchanged cards, and I had promised to do my utmost to help Brian achieve his objective. Was it the wine or was it my amazement at having encountered a hero of my childhood? Whatever, over the next few days I decided I must do something.

I agonized over this for some days before deciding to invite a few financial experts, who happened to be friends, to dinner. I explained during my telephone call to invite them that I would like to take their advice on charitable fundraising. No one seemed interested. I changed tactics: how would they like to have dinner with the famous Brian Rix? They all would!

And this is how I gathered together several city experts for dinner at the Chesterfield Hotel, Mayfair on July 8 1981.

Most encouraging of them was Edward Myatt who was founder and chairman of Intel Ltd. He had years of experience and at once not only grasped the challenge facing Brian but also proposed a solution. It was in two parts. First there would need to be an effective way of producing capital and second a vehicle for distributing it. The money-producing machine was to be the Mencap Unit Trust[126] – a unit trust formed in the ordinary way with investors able to keep any capital growth from their units, but they were to covenant their income (tax free) to the vehicle for distribution, which was to become the Mencap City Foundation.

Much work went into setting up the first ever charitable unit trust – an historic step in charitable fundraising. Permission was required from all and sundry, including the Department of Trade and Industry, as well as the Inland Revenue. Lawyers, bankers, investment managers, and accountants spent many hours leading up to the launch, which was generously underwritten by Sir Mark Weinberg.[127]

---

126 Later developed into the United Charities Unit Trust in 1987.
127 Sir Mark Aubrey Weinberg (born 1931) a founder of Abbey Life Assurance Company.

The great day arrived on March 31 1982 for the public launch by the then Chancellor of the Exchequer, Sir Geoffrey Howe,[128] but as Brian reported in his autobiography:

> There was only one snag. He launched it on the day the Argentines invaded the Falklands. The media had eyes for little else ...[129]

Despite this apparent setback, the serious financial media took up the theme of this new and unique unit trust, and it was enthusiastically endorsed by brokers and investors who, incidentally, benefited from substantial capital growth while deriving satisfaction from being able to assist so worthy a cause as Mencap.

The City Foundation had held its inaugural meeting as early as January 25 1982 and was more than ready to receive regular income from the unit trust and to distribute it to the numerous beneficiaries.

As the trustees of the foundation, we met twice yearly to consider a wide variety of applicants, all under the careful supervision of the administrating governor, Loretto Lamb. Significant contributions to these lengthy meetings were made by the late Roger Paul, a wonderful friend from Suffolk, and the late Helmut Rothenberg,[130] one of Mencap's most generous donors throughout his distinguished professional life.

Several millions of pounds resulted from that fateful meeting on the train. Why? Because neither Brian nor I had missed an opportunity. It would have been so easy to go our separate ways with nothing resulting. A *significance* in events? Yes, I think so.

Wherever Brian is, there is never a dull moment, and despite his initial hundred per cent concentration on securing Mencap's finances, Brian always had time for other interests into which he poured his boundless energy and enthusiasm.

One of my major interests at the time was developing the English Speaking Union in East Anglia. I was always looking out for entertaining

---

128 Richard Edward Geoffrey Howe, Baron Howe of Aberavon (born 1926), a former British conservative politician.
129 Brian Rix, *Face About Farce*, page 132
130 Founder of city accountants Blick, Rothenberg and Noble.

speakers for regional events, and who could be more appropriate than Brian Rix?

We decided to make a weekend of it. On the Friday was the official dinner at which Brian held a hundred guests enthralled, brilliantly putting in a punch line or two at the end about our responsibility to the mentally disabled. All were entertained and challenged at the same time. On Saturday, a few guests gathered round my table for a long leisurely luncheon and a time of well-deserved relaxation for Brian and Elspeth.[131] On Sunday morning, I looked through my bedroom window to see Brian strolling round the lawn in his dressing gown. What a lot had been achieved, I thought, since I first saw him on stage at the Whitehall Theatre thirty years before. And I had discovered that the "King of Farce" was a serious and practical humanitarian.

---

131 Elspeth Jean Gray, Lady Rix, née Mac Gregor-Gray (born 1929), a Scottish actress, known for her work on British television in the 1970s and '80s.

16: Harold Macmillan

Maurice Harold Macmillan, 1ˢᵗ Earl of Stockton, OM, PC

In the early 1980s I was active in the Conservative Party. Consequently, I often stayed in the Carlton Club, called by some the unofficial party headquarters.

One evening I noticed an aging Harold Macmillan[132] hobble into the morning room. Sitting down, he sipped a glass of port whilst just gazing ahead. I was aware that he was almost blind and could only read large-print books, of which there were none to hand, and that he frequently stayed at the club for several days at a time since the death of his wife.[133]

I walked over to him.

"So good to see you, Sir. How is Lady Blanche?" I had decided on this approach, as I was not sure he would recognize me. Lady Blanche[134] was his sister-in-law and a neighbour and friend in East Anglia.

"She is well, but her guests last weekend were rather dull. I'm not interested in football.[135] In future I will insist on knowing who her guests will be before accepting."

Thereupon we agreed that "Lady Blanche" would be our code to allow him to recognize me as his blindness advanced.

After this initial encounter, I enjoyed several conversations with the former prime minister. One of the longest was when he invited me to join him for dinner at Buck's, one of his many clubs.

---

132 Maurice Harold Macmillan, 1ˢᵗ Earl of Stockton (1894–1986), was prime minister of the United Kingdom from 10 January 1957 to 18 October 1963.
133 Lady Dorothy Macmillan (1900–66).
134 Lady Blanche Cobbold (1898–1987)
135 Lady Blanche Cobbold was President of Ipswich Town Football Club.

"Are you free to join me for dinner?" he asked me at about 7 p.m. one evening.

Actually, I had already made an arrangement to dine with an old friend who, I felt, would understand that I could hardly turn down such a unique opportunity to dine alone with "Super Mac" as he was known, I think, in America, where he was close friends with Kennedy.[136] My friend at once urged me to accompany Macmillan and to be sure to report back next day.

Most of the conversation, or at least the part I remember, was about religion. He had clearly suffered a great deal of stress in his early years especially over the well-known "affair" of his wife with Bob Boothby.[137] Macmillan was puritanical in his attitude to questions of sexual morality, and his wife's behaviour had caused him a great deal of anguish. In addition, Macmillan was increasingly drawn to Roman Catholicism and might well have converted had he not felt it would have gone against his "establishment" outlook. He spoke warmly of Ronald Knox,[138] who had often stayed with him at 10 Downing Street in his final months there. He said Knox was ready to receive him into the Roman Church.

After dinner, we slowly ascended the stairs leading to the drawing room on the landing, where Macmillan wanted to show me a remarkable entry in an old membership application book.

"Look here, dear boy, at this page." I was amazed to see that long ago he had been proposed for membership of Buck's only to be rejected as "unsuitable".

"That was when I was a young man, and my father was in trade, you see," he said rather wistfully. His father had, in fact, been a successful publisher, starting the famous firm MacMillan & Co. Ltd. However, in those days he was clearly not grand enough, and perhaps all his life he had an unconscious inferiority complex because of this.

---

136 John Fitzgerald "Jack" Kennedy (1917–1963) was the 35th President of the United States, serving from 1961 until his assassination in 1963.
137 Robert John Graham Boothby, Lord Boothby (1900–86) was a British Conservative politician. The affair lasted nearly thirty years.
138 Father Ronald Arbuthnott Knox (1888–1957) was an English Roman Catholic theologian, priest, and crime writer.

Of course, once he had married an Earl's daughter and become a prominent politician, Buck's welcomed him with open arms – and hence my very first memorable visit to that club.

Towards the end of his life I mostly met Harold Macmillan over breakfast, and I knew his blindness was complete when he asked me to butter his toast. He had very little left but his memories of momentous events and remarkable characters on the world's stage.

Once in the early hours of the morning, I crept towards my room in pitch darkness. I felt for my bed, ready to collapse into it, when to my astonishment I felt a foot protruding out of the bed. It was clearly not my room! With horror I realized I had entered Harold Macmillan's room. Luckily, he did not stir and I slowly crept out into my own room next door.

In those days, the club bedrooms were unlocked with no security even for a former prime minister.

17: Terence Amerasinghe

Dr Terence Amerasinghe

Words are entirely inadequate to describe the multi-talented Terence Amerasinghe.

I first heard his name from Alan Lee-Williams[139] (then Director General of the English Speaking Union). Alan gave me Terence's card. At that time I was interested in Sri Lanka's sapphires, which were thought by experts to be the best in the world, and I decided to visit Sri Lanka. In my pocket I carried Terence's card.

After a week's preoccupation with sapphires, I telephoned Dr Amerasinghe. His response was "We have met before." At first I thought that there was some esoteric inference in these words! However, upon meeting our hero by the swimming pool of Colombo's Intercontinental Hotel, I learned the truth. By some strange fate Terence had been seated immediately behind me on the BA flight from London and had listened to my every word throughout the journey of twelve hours!

Through this meeting, the ESU of Sri Lanka was born.

It is no exaggeration to say that meeting Terence changed the focus of my life for the next twenty years. He influenced me to understand the importance of English in the context of Sri Lanka's ethnic crisis.

The arrangement was this. Terence would dedicate his time to establishing the ESU of Sri Lanka. I would get the support of the ESU in the UK and arrange funding. This was made easier as at the time I was chairman of the East Region of the ESU and a governor of the ESU of the Commonwealth.

---

139 Alan Lee Williams (born 1930) was a former president of the Atlantic Treaty Association, a British Labour Party politician, writer, and visiting professor of politics at Queen Mary College, London. In 1979, he was appointed Director General of the English Speaking Union.

My meeting with Terence by the swimming pool was on September 30 1981. By the middle of October, he reported that he had enlisted the first seventeen members. A committee had been formed, and he had been elected president. On 11 November, President J.R. Jayewardene had agreed to be patron. HRH Prince Philip (President of the ESU of the Commonwealth) sent a telegram of congratulations, and the American ambassador joined the organization.

In 1982 London paid tribute to the new ESU of Sri Lanka by holding a dinner at Dartmouth House hosted by the then chairman, Sir Patrick Dean[140] and attended by the Sri Lankan High Commissioner and many leading members of the diplomatic community.

Terence worked long hours. He began classes in elementary English based on the Callan method, both in Colombo and Kandy. He trained teachers in this method himself. Over the following ten years, over 5,000 young students, mostly from the poorest sectors of society, learned to speak basic English, thus enabling themselves to get jobs in hotels and as taxi drivers, hospital attendants, and receptionists.

Once a year an Awards Day was held, at which students demonstrated their new-found skills and at which guests of honour included the Prime Minister, the ex-President, cabinet ministers, ambassadors and so on.

A library was established, and the UK East Region contributed 1,000 books. Director General David Hicks[141] and other UK leaders visited Sri Lanka to encourage the work. A newspaper was published regularly, called *Open Mind*, written, edited, and printed by Terence.

The great day came for the grand opening of the HQ of the organization in 1989. It was opened by President Premadasa with ex-President J.R. Jayewardene by his side. Only Terence could get two presidents at once to such an occasion attended by half the cabinet! I and Major Anthony Gurney[142] represented the ESU UK. Both presidents are now dead – Premadasa assassinated soon afterwards by his own bodyguard.

---

140 Sir Patrick Henry Dean (1909–1994) was Permanent Representative of the United Kingdom to the United Nations from 1960 to 1964 and British Ambassador to the United States from 1965 to 1969.
141 David Hicks was Director General of ESU 1989-91.
142 See chapter 6

As I got to know Terence, I quickly realized that the ESU was just one activity in which he enthusiastically engaged himself. I also realized that all his activity was related to his core belief. He really believed in the "Brotherhood of Man", and he was never afraid to stand up for his beliefs. He was one of those rare souls born to challenge his fellow men, even if it made them a little uncomfortable. Utterly secure within himself, he feared no one. He carried on with his work oblivious to worldly cares and comforts, though he enjoyed his daily glass of whisky and endless cigarettes, like Churchill defying all medical advice and living long to tell the tale!

Terence was a tireless worker who could not comprehend laziness. His work was joy and his relaxation stimulating conversation. And what an intellect! I envied his clarity of thought, his impressive memory, and his analytical honesty.

His understanding of literature, especially poetry, was equalled in my experience only by the late Sir George Trevelyan.[143] Literature to both men was a means to an end, never an end in itself. Terence felt that the great poets expressed the vision of man's unfulfilled potential.

On one occasion, Terence was challenged to take part in a poetry competition at an English university. Without warning, the participants had to quote a verse of a poem containing a female name beginning with each letter from A to Z. Terence used to love to recount how he began with "Annabel Lee" (Edgar Allan Poe) and continued right through the alphabet to "Zenocrate" (Christopher Marlow). I can hear him now:

"Ah fair Zenocrate, divine Zenocrate,
Fair is too foul an epithet for thee."

He did not miss out a letter and thus won the competition against leading UK literates, and he went on for many years to regale his friends with his recitation into the night hours.

I have kept every letter that Terence sent me since October 1981 until his last letter of January this year. There are over 500. How I wish I had taken some of his advice more seriously, for he was very wise. However I have those letters, a literary goldmine, to read and reread.

---

143 See chapter 3

I owe Terence a great deal, especially his introduction to President Jayewardene who became a close friend and mentor. How fortunate I am to have known such giants among men.

It is very difficult to sum up such a varied yet focused life.

Terence could be difficult. He had little time for superficial small talk or for those who did not consistently share his enthusiasm or his preoccupations. He was, however, loyal to those he trusted, even when, as in my case, they did not always live up to his expectations. Gentlemen – and such was he – hold loyalty as the highest of virtues.

Terence expected much, and therefore I wonder if he was secretly disappointed by the slow response of others to his challenge. If so, he did not show it. He revealed to the world only the consistency of his beliefs matched by his actions.

One of my fondest memories is of a clear starlit night. We were sitting on the terrace of a hotel in Kandy. We had dined well – Terence on the hottest available curry to which he had added a liberal dose of Tabasco. We settled down to a bottle of whisky and a box of cigars. For several hours we discussed history and philosophy and the state of the modern world and addressed the question – is there hope for mankind?

Terence expanded his views at length and began to convince me that there is hope, but at a price. The price is the giving up of narrow views and egocentric behaviour in favour of a willingness to open up to others with complete trust however alien they may seem. By then it was 4 a.m., and I was half asleep. These thoughts, however, slipped deeply into my mind that night and have never left me.

Terence has left many of us with a legacy of deeply held convictions with practical applications, as for example in his work for the ESU. I know of several whose lives were changed for the better by knowing Terence and who now follow in his footsteps in their determination to build a better world. His influence lives on, and our best tribute to this giant amongst men is to emulate his example in our own way and thus protect his legacy.

Terence was the supreme optimist. His last handwritten letter to me is dated 13 January 2007. He was ninety. He wrote:

This year I have two things planned. We are holding a seminar in Greece in March. I might take an extra week there because the climate is wonderful and some investors want to examine the land. The olive season was on and we made 5,000 euro from our crop! I am using this to refurbish the place – especially communication wise, computer, fax etc.

In June to Togo ...

But it was not to be. At the end of May he felt ill in Sri Lanka. He instinctively rushed to the airport and boarded a plane for Canada to join his daughter. Soon after arriving, he was admitted to hospital. His son-in-law, Chandra Krishnaratne reports:

In the very early morning of June 1st he said goodbye to all of us; he shook my hand for the very last time as he was wheeled into the operating theatre, a smile on his face. He was a man who never complained of anything. He never said anything negative.

What an example!

18: J.R. Jayewardene

Junius Richard Jayewardene, first Executive President of Sri Lanka

*I*n 1984, together with Dr Terence Amerasinghe.[144] I ascended the wide marble staircase in President's House, Colombo to be greeted by an impressive tall figure in a white sarong extending a welcoming hand and smiling broadly. It was the famous J.R.

Junius Richard Jayewardene, always known as J.R., had been president of Sri Lanka for six years since February 1978. A natural leader, he had held most of the important offices of state, including prime minister, and now presided over a flourishing economy that was attracting significant investors from around the globe.

I was one of the smallest of them! I had first gone to Sri Lanka in search of the famous blue sapphires and, initially successful, had invested some of the proceeds from the sale of those stones into two ventures – Lanka Carbons, a factory that produced high quality carbon from coconut husks, and a small farm.

It was, however, not as an investor that I ascended the stairs but as cofounder, with Dr Amerasinghe, of the Sri Lankan branch of the English Speaking Union (ESU).[145]

J.R. had without hesitation agreed to be patron of the new Sri Lankan ESU and clearly took his patronage seriously. Before our meeting, he had requested a detailed report of progress so far and was well prepared to question and advise us.

"My English may not be perfect. Perhaps you detect a slight accent? You see my nanny was Scottish!" He spoke warmly of his memories of

---

144 See chapter 17
145 The English Speaking Union, an international educational organization founded by the journalist Sir John Evelyn Leslie Wrench (1882–1966) in 1918.

Miss Monroe, who had somehow found her way from the cold north of Scotland to the markedly warmer climes of Sri Lanka.

J.R. seemed to be completely at ease as he led the conversation in perfect English and enthusiastically pledged his support for our endeavours. He spoke of his appreciation of a telegram he had received from Prince Philip, President of the International ESU, whom he had known and, he said, admired for many years.

That evening I received a telephone call from the presidential secretary, Mr de Silva.

"Forgive me, but His Excellency has asked me to ascertain your age. He guesses about 70."

"Good Heavens!" I replied. "I am thirty-nine. Why does he think I am so old?"

"Well, because you have achieved so much. That's why!"

I suppose it was a sort of compliment. Over the next five years I was privileged to have many encounters with J.R., most of them at his delightful villa in Ward Place, which, for the uninitiated, is in the fashionable part of Colombo, rather like Eaton Square in London.

Towards the end of 1988, J.R. was faced with a major challenge. Should he finally retire as president? He had endorsed a new constitution allowing for the president to serve just two terms. Now his second term was up.

"What do you think, Wynne-Parker?"

"Well, Sir, if you wish to remain in good standing with the British Commonwealth and Her Majesty, you have no choice. You must retire and make way for your successor."

"But who? But who? That is my problem?"

There was the well-liked candidate of the establishment, Lalith Athulathmudali,[146] and another populist Ranasinghe Premadasa.[147]

"I suggest you go for Premadasa, Sir," I ventured. "He is a man of the people. They respect and identity with him."

---

146 Lalith William Samarasekera Athulathmudali (1936–1993) was a Sri Lankan politician of the United National Party and a former cabinet minister of Trade, National Security, Agriculture, Education and deputy minister of Defence.

147 Ranasinghe Premadasa (1924–1993) was the third president of Sri Lanka from January 2 1989 to May 1 1993. Before that, he served as the prime minister in the government headed by J. R. Jayewardene from February 6 1978 to January 1 1989.

J.R. was finally convinced and thereafter wholly endorsed Premadasa. I may or may not have had undue influence over this decision, but speculation was rife, and *The Sunday Times* (of Sri Lanka) referred on its front page to "frequent meetings at Ward Place, attended among others by Michael Wynne-Parker, we *believe*, in an informal capacity." [148]

This was not the interpretation of the British Foreign Office who instructed the ambassador, David Gladstone,[149] to enquire what Wynne-Parker was up to!

Premadasa succeeded J.R. as president in January 1989. I received a call from J.R. "Michael, I have suggested to my successor that he should receive you tomorrow morning at his private residence. Please be ready. A car will collect you at 5 a.m.!"

At 5 a.m. sharp I was at the door of the Oberoi Hotel. A car with police escort arrived promptly, and I set off to the outskirts of Colombo, where President Premadasa had his private quarters.

High walls surrounded the President's compound. The car paused at the gates, and in the still dark early morning I could hear an exchange of voices. The gates opened, the car door was almost immediately opened, and I was escorted along a sandy path, up some steps, and into a candle-lit chamber. In the distance I saw what I thought was the figure of Premadasa, and I marched forward extending my hand, only to find it was a life sized "cut out" of the President, probably left over from his election campaign! Feeling rather stupid, I was led over to a table clearly set out for breakfast.

No sooner had I sat down than in walked the real president grinning broadly. I rose.

"I thought that might fool you!" he said.

We shook hand and sat down. During the short breakfast he told me that he had heard about the ESU and that he wholeheartedly supported its aims and would give all possible assistance.

I later telephoned J.R.

"How do you think I did?"

---

148 *The Sunday Times*, September 18 1988
149 David Arthur Stewart Gladstone, CMG (born 1935) High Commissioner to Sri Lanka 1987–91.

"Splendid!" said J.R. "Especially that bit where you told him he was the Thatcher of Asia."

I had said this because, like Margaret Thatcher, Premadasa needed only four hours sleep – hence our early breakfast. In fact, he became famous for calling cabinet members at 4.30 in the morning.

Thanks to J.R., I became quite close to his successor over the next few years.

On 26 June 1990, a newspaper reporter rushed up to me in the foyer of the Oberoi Hotel, Colombo.

"Have you heard the news, Sir? A bomb has almost destroyed the Carlton Club in London."[150]

My first reaction was to say that if I had not been in Colombo, I might well have been attending a dinner there. My second reaction was to say, "Well, I feel safer in Colombo."

This was reported in the next morning's *Daily News* and was music in the ears of Premadasa! At 9 a.m. I received a telephone call from the President's secretary inviting me to attend the opening ceremony of a "Village Awakening[151]" near Kandy.

"The President would like to thank you personally for your words."

After the long journey from Colombo, I arrived at Kandy to be received by the President's daughter and son-in-law who looked after me attentively until the ceremony began.

At 8 p.m. the President arrived, the trumpeters sounded their welcome, and a thousand dancers appeared, exotically clad, to the hypnotic sound of drums. I was seated next to the President who clapped in rhythm to the beat of the drums. Turning to me he said, "You did more good to assure people of the safety of our land than all the expensive efforts of the British PR firm. Thank you."

Though touched by his kind words, I had a more pressing concern. The back legs of my chair were slowly but surely sinking into the soft

---

[150] At 8.39 pm on 25 June 1990, the Carlton Club was bombed by the Provisional Irish Republican Army (IRA), injuring more than 20 people. Lord Kaberry later died of his injuries received in the attack.

[151] In 1978 the village of Kukulewa, in the North Central Province of Sri Lanka, was selected for development under the Gam Udava (Village Awakening) program launched by the recently elected UNP (United National Party) government.

ground, and I had to move gradually forward perching on the front of the chair to avoid ending up in a very undignified position!

J.R. was not the sort of man to retire. I sometimes thought that Premadasa exercised considerable patience with the continued and rather prominent involvement of his predecessor in the political and cultural life of the capital. There were in effect two presidents – one in power and one with influence.

One day J.R. invited me to lunch at Ward Place, asking me to arrive early before the rest of his guests.

"You once told me of a special drink enjoyed by the Queen Mother, and I want you to describe it to my butler, and he will serve it to all my guests."

"I hope, Sir, your butler has the necessary gin and Dubonnet?"

"If not, he will find it, which is why I wanted you to arrive early."

On arrival, each guest was handed a chilled glass of two parts gin and one part Dubonnet. Most of the guests were Buddhists and not great drinkers and certainly not used to taking two or three stiff drinks *before* luncheon.

As half of Premadasa's cabinet sat down, a very jolly lunch followed at which J.R. exerted his customary control without a murmur of dissent.

"Very good, Wynne-Parker. Just like the old days," said J.R. in a low voice. I was on his right.

"Very bad," said Gladstone[152] opposite me and the only other Englishman present. "What would the Foreign Office think of this?"

I spent many happy and informative evenings with J.R. following his official retirement. We sat in his garden smoking fine Cohiba cigars. This was the first time I had smoked a Cohiba, and I commented on its excellence.

"There is a story here," said the great man. "I was invited to Cuba on a state visit. Of course I was interested to meet Fidel Castro,[153] but I was worried about how we would get on. I am a capitalist and he

---

152 H.E. David Gladstone (born 1935) British High Commissioner to Sri Lanka 1987-91.
153 Fidel Alejandro Castro Ruz (born 1926), a Cuban politician and former president, leader of the Cuban Revolution.

is a communist, so we had very little in common. Castro, however, immediately put me at ease. In fact, in private he has a charming and easy manner. He offered me a cigar. It was my first Cohiba. Smoking it was sheer pleasure, and I complimented him on its flavour."

"You are a connoisseur, Sir," said Castro. "Unfortunately, Prince Charles did not enjoy these specially produced cigars, so I saved them for you."

Such was the rapport created between these disparate leaders through their mutual appreciation of the world's best cigar that the communist Castro sent the capitalist Jayewardene a box of twenty-five Cohibas each month thereafter. Thus, he had built up quite a stock. J.R. told me that he used to keep a box of the cigars on his cabinet table.[154]

"Gamini,[155] do you agree with my estimated budget?"

"Yes, Sir."

"Very good. Have a cigar."

"Nissanka,[156] do you agree with my proposals?"

"Yes, Sir."

"Have a cigar."

This story of J.R.'s state visit to Cuba prompted an increasingly favourite theme.

"Wynne-Parker."

"Yes, Sir."

"Can you arrange a state visit to the United Kingdom?"

"Well, Sir, you are now no longer head of state."

"No matter. You have the influence. I missed two state visits due to our Tamil riots and your elections. I would dearly love to see the Queen – and Margaret Thatcher."

"Sir, a state visit is out of the question, but an *informal* visit, which can include the Queen and Prime Minister, is, of course, possible, but there will be no horse-drawn carriage procession down the Mall, I'm afraid."

---

154 How Churchill would have appreciated this and what a far cry from the tedious political correctness of today!
155 Lionel Gamini Dissanayake (1942–94) was a prominent Sri Lankan politician and a former presidential candidate and leader of the opposition.
156 Deshamanya Nissanka Parakrama Wijeyeratne (1924–2007) was a Sri Lankan politician, civil servant and diplomat. See chapter 19

Back in London I had much to do. I needed a main reason for J.R.'s visit. Suddenly it occurred to me. Every year was held a Commonwealth inter-faith service at Westminster Abbey, the highlight of the Commonwealth year. But what if we were to inaugurate an annual Commonwealth lecture? I immediately telephoned Sir Donald Tebbit[157] and Sir Peter Marshall[158] who took enthusiastically to the idea.

November 15 1989 was the proposed date, and J.R. approved.

A call to Sir William Heseltine[159] confirmed that Her Majesty would be delighted to receive J.R., and Margaret Thatcher was equally enthusiastic.

On November 14 began J.R.'s unofficial "state visit" to Britain. He stayed at Claridge's at his request and was accompanied by his wife, grandson, doctor, and secretary.

November 15 was an exhausting day. An interview with *The Times* was followed by a luncheon at the Carlton Club for the ESU of South Asia and then by tea with Margaret Thatcher at 10 Downing Street.[160] Then came a short rest back at Claridge's before the inaugural lecture introduced by Lord Pym.[161]

"Mr President," he said. "I congratulate you on your spoken English and wonder where you acquired such a skill?"

J.R. rose to reply. "Lord Pym, I acquired it in the same way as you, on my nanny's knee – but twenty years before you were born!"

Few before then had heard of the President's famous Scottish nanny Miss Monroe, but the main point of that lecture was the universality of the common language – English being as much the language of a Buddhist Sri Lankan as of a Christian Englishman. J.R. emphasized that he had learned through bitter experience that the absence of a common language led to lack of communication and civil war.

---

157 Sir Donald Tebbit (1920–2010) was a British diplomat, chief clerk of the Foreign and Commonwealth Office from 1972 to 1976, and British High Commissioner to Australia from 1976 to 1980.

158 Sir Peter Marshall, a British diplomat and former Commonwealth Deputy Secretary-General (1983-88).

159 Sir William Frederick Payne Heseltine (born 1930) was private secretary to Queen Elizabeth II from 1986 to 1990.

160 See chapter 22

161 Francis Leslie Pym (1922–1983) was secretary of state for Foreign and Commonwealth Affairs.

On November 16, we were received at Buckingham Palace by Prince Philip, and at midday Sir Guy Acland[162] announced that Her Majesty was ready to receive J.R., whose wife was also welcomed in time for luncheon.

After the formal events in London, the former first couple visited us in rural Norfolk. My daughter Fiona well remembers the visit. She presented J.R. with her pet rabbit, who left an indelible stain on the President's immaculate white sarong!

On Sunday 19 November, we lunched with Anthony and Patricia Gurney[163] at Northrepps, where J.R. took a great interest in the famous cattle herd. *The Eastern Daily Press* took up the story:[164]

> A tiny village in North Norfolk played host to a world leader yesterday – and it could pave the way for a herd of local cows to be exported to Asia.
>
> President Jayewardene of Sri Lanka, the longest serving leader of a Commonwealth Country, visited Northrepps, two miles south-east of Cromer. His visit was shrouded in secrecy because of tight security.[165]
>
> After meeting the Queen and the Prime Minister earlier this week, he dropped in far an informal lunch at Manor Farm, home of Major Anthony Gurney.
>
> The President, who has been in politics for 52 years, then looked at a herd of pedigree Friesian cows which will be airlifted to his country around March 1990.

J.R. had noticed a small figure of a Buddha in Anthony Gurney's dining room which had been discovered in Rangoon.

---

162 Lieutenant-Colonel Sir Christopher Guy Dyke Acland, 6th Baronet (born 1946) a British Army officer and member of the British royal household..
163 See chapter 6.
164 E.D.P. November 20 1989.
165 Because of several threats from the rebel Tamil Tigers.

"A very good sign," said J.R. "You will return to the East and to Sri Lanka."

And indeed, very soon afterwards Anthony Gurney did so, not just because of the cattle, but as a leading supporter of the ESU. He attended the opening ceremony of the ESU headquarters in Colombo on February 6 1990 by the two presidents – J.R. acting as the ever-charming host and Premadasa, the actual head of state, as honoured guest.

19: Nissanka Wijeyeratne

Deshamanya Dr Nissanka Parakrama Wijeyeratne

*L*ike his compatriot *J.R. Jayewardene*, Nissanka was a Buddhist with an appreciation of Christianity.

"Civilization is made up of several great religions," he said. "The most important aspect for civilized men and women is respect – respect for another's point of view whilst holding one's own belief sincerely."

Nissanka did not believe in ecumenism or the gradual blending of different faiths. He believed in distinctive paths to be trodden thoughtfully and tolerantly.

We had many interesting discussions mostly during my frequent visits to Sri Lanka in the 1980s when Nissanka held the important office of Minister of Justice in J.R.'s[166] cabinet.

Once in 1985 he turned up in my suite at the Oberoi Hotel for lunch looking very worried.

"You see, this afternoon I have to sign four execution orders, and both as a Buddhist and as a man, I do not really believe in the death penalty. Yet I have to do it as part of my ministerial function."

And he could not bring himself to resign. There was a part of him that loved public office and, I suppose, the power that goes with it.

He looked the part, always dressed traditionally in his white sarong and sporting a silk Hermes scarf. Dignified of manner, he was careful in speech and a quiet but commanding presence.

He was from an old Kandyan family, a descendent of the ancient kings who ruled the Singala Island race three thousand years ago. He

---

166 Junius Richard Jayewardene (1906–1996) famously abbreviated in Sri Lanka as J.R., was the first Executive President of Sri Lanka, serving from 1978 till 1989. See chapter 18.

was a proud yet humble man, as was revealed when he once escorted me to the Hill Club, Nurelia.

He said, "You British established this club – so exclusive that until recently you, an Englishman, could be a full member but I, a Sri Lankan, even as Minister of Justice, could only enter as your guest."

This he stated as a matter of fact and without an ounce of resentment. People of old cultures do not become mean-spirited under occupation.

Nissanka, though a philosopher and poet,[167] was a workaholic. He lived in Kandy and left by chauffeur-driven Mercedes at 6 a.m. to arrive at 10 a.m. in his office in Colombo. Late in the evening and often after an official dinner, he would usually return.

For ten years he held the almost hereditary position of Keeper of the Temple of the Tooth in Kandy. This ancient shrine houses one of the Buddha's teeth. One day I was privileged to be taken up a winding staircase into the holiest part of the shrine to see this ancient relic that was usually concealed under a sevenfold canopy. Nissanka took his position as Keeper of the Tooth very seriously and regarded it as more important than his ministerial post.

Anyone visiting Kandy is struck by the beauty and tranquillity of its location, which is why Lord Mountbatten,[168] then Supreme Commander of the Allied Forces in South Asia, located the British operational headquarters there in 1944. Many a British officer has relaxed in the lush botanical gardens reminiscent of the garden landscapes of his native land.

From the moment Dr Amerasinghe[169] and I began the English Speaking Union in Sri Lanka, we could count on Nissanka's staunch support quite beyond the call of duty. Despite his incredibly busy life, he attended almost all our events – lectures, receptions and dinners – and thereby influenced other important potential supporters.

He sometimes visited London, and I tried to repay something of his generosity to me in Colombo. Of course, he loved traditional British ways; he had been partly brought up with them being educated at Royal

---

167 *Ape Appacci: An Anthology of Our Father's Poems*, published in 2001.
168 Louis Francis Albert Victor Nicholas George Mountbatten, 1st Earl Mountbatten of Burma (1900–79) was a British Admiral of the Fleet and statesman of German descent. He was the last Viceroy of the British Indian Empire (1947).
169 See chapter 17

College Colombo. I took him to lunch and dine at my clubs, always immaculately turned out in his native attire.

Then he asked me to take him to Annabel's. Walking in, we met Lady Rothermere[170] standing by the central bar.

"How nice to see you, Michael! Do, please, introduce me to your Arab Sheikh."

"You had better be careful, Patricia," I replied. "He is not an Arab Sheikh but Minister of Justice of Sri Lanka – with the power of life and death."

---

170 Patricia Evelyn Beverley Matthews Harmsworth, Viscountess Rothermere (1933–1992) was an English socialite and actress, known to her intimate circle as Bubbles.

20: Dai Llewelyn

Sir David St Vincent "Dai" Llewellyn, 4th Baronet

Dai was one of those characters who appear to have no beginning and no end. Certainly, I cannot remember a time in London when he was not around. And his spirit remains.

He died prematurely, and, though he had been seriously ill with bone cancer for some time, I was shocked when I saw his picture in the *Daily Mail* of November 22 2008. That thin haggard face bore no resemblance to Dai. It was handed to me by Luigi,[171] our thoughtful hall porter at the Cavalry & Guards Club on my arrival home after several weeks abroad. Being away, I had missed the rumours apparently circulating in London that he was ill, so I was unprepared for what I was to read in that long article headed "I did it Dai's way". The article indicated that he had only a little time left but did not reveal where he was – just "in a hospice", and a hospice is a one-way house.

At once I rang Steve Metcalfe, another friend of Dai's, who somehow found the address of the hospice and suggested we drive there together next day.

The picture had not lied. At the hospice resided a ghost of the former man, extending a shaking hand of surprised welcome.

"Have a drink. It's only 11 a.m., but never too early," squeaked an unfamiliar voice as he pointed to a cupboard. Steve and I were too shocked to refuse and gulped down a sustaining glass of red wine.

Of course, it was excessive drink that was killing our friend who had never been able to say "no". I had known several heavy drinkers, but no one matched Dai's capacity.

---

171 Luigi Ciortan

He seemed not to have any regrets, and pointing to the only photograph on the bedside window of his brother Roddy, he declared that after many acrimonious years they had just been fully reconciled and that he could die in peace.

What a very good thing it was that I had seen that newspaper, thanks to Luigi, spoken with Steve, and travelled to see Dai, for he died just a few days later.

For any reader who may not have known him, Dai is easy to describe – a big man physically and mentally, exuding endless enthusiasm and vigour. Very attractive to ladies and companionable with men, he was a "good sport" as they used to say. His facial expressions revealed a deep-seated humour and an attitude of amazement at the enchantments of life, especially so after he developed the distinctive Salvador Dali look.

Behind this air of *joie de vivre* and despite his fame as a "playboy" (or in politer circles a socialite), there were deeper aspects to him. He went off on secret charitable ventures, for instance, driving relief convoys in Yugoslavia.[172] He also held a sincere political belief in keeping the United Kingdom as free as possible from the sinister tentacles of Brussels. And he never complained or revealed the mystery of the abject poverty that stalked his final years.

On the surface Dai seemed unchanged. Always immaculately dressed, sporting a red rose in his lapel button-hole, marching with his usual confidence into his London clubs, no one could have guessed that he had spent the previous night in the dormitory of a local hostel for the down and out.

It was not only excessive drinking that had financially ruined him but also gambling. Though never in the big league of gamblers, simply because he rarely had very much money, he could not resist the temptation of playing that last hand or placing the last chip.

One evening I mat a joyous Dai walking into the Clermont Club.

"My dear boy, how good to see you. I've just been paid two thousand pounds for a television interview. Let's celebrate!"

It was impossible to influence him to save at least half of the money. He was well known in the club, where he had been social secretary

---

172 In 1992

when I first knew him, and temporally affluent, we were pampered by an attentive staff in that splendid dining room from which, several bottles of wine later, Dai ascended the elegant staircase to the gaming rooms above.

Serious gamblers do not like to be watched, and I remained downstairs reading the day's newspapers – but not for long.

"Well I'm cleaned out, dear boy," said a red-faced Dai. "Be a good chap and lend me a tenner for the taxi home."

Of course, he was not going home. For Dai was a man of the night. Usually rising as late as possible, his first perfect appointment would be a good late lunch where he would linger over glasses of wine or cognac until one by one his hosts would have to leave. Later, refreshed and changed (somehow, somewhere), Dai would begin his evenings as we had done at the Clermont, before going on finally to those establishments that close somewhere between dawn and breakfast time.

Dai was an amazing example of someone who lived very well on very little. The secret was that he was very good with people, empathizing readily with most of those he met. He had the gift of making friends who never deserted him and helped him, sensitively, according to their means. His constant communications, telephone calls, postcards from exotic places – one could never forget him.

And he was a thoughtful introducer. Once sitting next to him at a friend's dinner, he said he would like to introduce me to someone with whom I would have much in common that very night. Bidding a hasty farewell to our hosts, Dai led me through Berkeley Square to Aspinalls where I met Jafar Ramini.

"Jafar, my old bean, meet Michael Wynne-Parker, another Welsh cousin and friend of the Arabs." With that, Dai left (upstairs for the gaming tables, of course).

Now if Dai was a novice gambler, Jafar was the professional having played for some of the highest stakes with some of the world's biggest punters. Years before, he had arrived in London from Palestine and had established himself as a leading member of both the Arab and British communities. Of course, with my lifelong passion for the Arabs and their culture, we had a great deal in common and instantly became friends – all due to Dai.

Several obituaries have endeavoured to sum up Dai's life with very great difficulty, even in attempting to answer the question, what did he do?

Of course he did "things" and attempted to "do" others. Perhaps he excelled best as director of the Dorchester Club, which at one stage became so successful that it even began to tempt Annabel's members to change loyalties! However, with all his other potentially permanent and lucrative positions, Dai somehow did not have the staying power, and soon that club was closed.

It was Mangal Kapoor who most accurately summed up our mutual friend in writing. "He kept up the façade of a high-rolling roué to the end but in truth he was a hard-up sponger ...[173]"

But *that* was not all. Dai was a devoted father and was liked by his daughters' contemporaries. At one Christmas dinner I asked my own youngest daughter,[174] then aged twenty, which guest out of about thirty she had enjoyed the company of most.

"Why, Dai of course. He took time to listen to me. Told me his favourite delicacy was badger claws just to wind me up! He made me laugh."

---

173 *Sunday Times*, January 18 2009
174 Fiona Wynne-Parker

21: Cecil Waidyaratne

General Cecil Waidyaratne

I met Cecil Waidyaratne in 1989 shortly after President Jayewardene's retirement as president. They were related by marriage.

"Not the easiest man to get on with," commented J.R., "but essentially the greatest of soldiers."

General Cecil Waidyaratne was born on 16 May 1938 and was educated at St Benedict's College, Colombo. He was an outstanding sportsman and represented the college in the cricket first eleven from 1956 to 1957. He loved his college and always rallied to the call of his Alma Mater.

He was enlisted in the regular force of the then Ceylon Army on June 26 1959. Having completed officer cadet training at the Royal Military Academy, Sandhurst, he was commissioned in the rank of second lieutenant on July 28 1961 and posted to the Ceylon Armoured Corps with effect from the same date.

Having earned due promotions, he rose to the rank of lieutenant colonel on January 1 1980 and was appointed commanding officer of the Sri Lanka Mechanical Engineers on the same date. Subsequently, he commanded 1st Battalion Sri Lanka Singha Regiment, 1st Reconnaissance Regiment Sri Lanka Armoured Corps, and 1st Battalion, the Rajarata Rifles. Thus, he had the rare opportunity of commanding four battalions. Further, he held the appointment of Commander Northern Area in 1985 and thereafter Southern Commander and General Officer Commanding 1 Division and also held the appointment of Commander of Combined Operations in 1989, and he was responsible for the security of the Colombo Metropolitan area.[175]

---

175 I am grateful to Major Mahesh de Zoysa his ADC for this information.

If My Table Could Talk

His strong personality mixed with intelligence and efficiency paved the way for his promotion to the rank of major general, upon which he was appointed chief of staff in 1989 about the time I got to know him. He was a colourful character with a colourful vocabulary, not afraid to speak his mind, ruthless, and at times impulsive.

Obtaining my telephone number from J.R., the General rang me in February 1990 to ask if we could meet in private. I invited him to dinner at the Oberoi. After several whiskies and well into the meal, he told me the following.

Two nights earlier, he was being driven along the Galle Face Green main road when his front escort outriders came to an abrupt halt. After a few moments and sensing there was no real danger, Cecil got out of his jeep to discover that the commotion was caused by two drunks refusing to move from the middle of the road.

"Have them arrested at once, and let us proceed," barked the infuriated General, who then continued to Army headquarters nearby.

Apparently the two drunks, who turned out to be British, were put in a local prison cell to cool down for the night. Coming round next morning, immediately upon release they contacted the British Embassy, complaining bitterly of their "torturous treatment". This treatment turned out to be no more than some harsh words and a very cold shower.

The British Embassy took a rather dim view of the situation, however, and a letter was sent from the High Commissioner David Gladstone,[176] to the President himself. And the President had asked the General for a written explanation and apology in English to the High Commissioner.

"The problem is," said Cecil, "though I can speak in English, I cannot write it."

And this is where I came in. Following dinner and over port and cigars was composed the following:

---

176 H.E. David Gladstone (born 1935) was British High Commissioner to Sri Lanka 1987-91.

Dear High Commissioner,

I understand that you felt my arrest of the two drunken Englishmen was of sufficient importance to write to the President.

Though I am sorry for any inconvenience caused to you, I can make no apology for rounding up two drunken and disorderly fellows who held up a busy General for several minutes, going about his lawful duty in the midst of a time of serious civil war …

Thus the General had both apologized and defended his behaviour, which greatly pleased the President. Indeed, on November 16 1991 he was promoted to Commander of the Army.[177]

After this, Cecil and I became firm friends. He was, naturally, extremely busy but also knew how to relax and enjoy himself, giving lively dinners at Army headquarters, where often his pet lion lay at his feet.

A lion was an appropriate pet for such a tough man. One of his favourite sayings was "A pack of camels led by a lion is far superior to a pack of lions led by a camel."

---

[177] Equivalent to Chief of the General Staff in the British Army.

22: Margaret Thatcher

Margaret Hilda Thatcher, Baroness Thatcher, LG, OM, PC, FRS

In August 1974 I was elected chairman of the Norwich Conservative candidates committee at the age of twenty-eight. I think it was a consolation prize for having been thoroughly beaten as Conservative candidate in the recent local elections. It was in that capacity that I received a telephone call from Central Office. It was to ask whether I would cast a vote for Margaret Thatcher in the forthcoming election for party leader. She was the only woman candidate and to most party traditionalists an outsider. Despite being not only a traditionalist but also rather a male chauvinist, some instinct caused me to pledge my support. And, for once, I backed the right horse! On 18 September 1975, Margaret Thatcher became the first woman leader of Her Majesty's opposition.

Fate played into her hands. Years of muddled government by both Labour and Conservatives had led Britain to crisis point, and the country was at the mercy of ruthless trade unions who respected none but their own.

Despite half-hearted support from many Conservatives, Thatcher rose to the occasion, and against almost impossible odds, she defeated the unions' iron grip and brought Britain back not only from the edge of the abyss but also onto the road towards stability. With stability, prosperity increased and renewed self-confidence.

Many of the old school could never come to terms with Margaret Thatcher. It was not just that they were unaccustomed to a woman at the helm. After all, the country was ruled by a wonderful queen, not to mention the nation's favourite grandmother, Queen Elizabeth. No, it was more to do with Margaret's inherent radicalism – and some snobbery; after all, she was just a grocer's daughter.

Ideologically Thatcher did not really fit into the traditional categories of "left" or "right". That is to say, she was the heir of neither the Whigs nor the Tories – those everlasting warring parties that had somehow evolved into the modern Conservative party. Thatcher was an outsider without whom, ironically, the party could neither hold together nor go on to achieve the power it was to maintain over three terms of office. Highly intelligent, well read, and a scientist, she was not basically an ideologue but a pragmatist. Yes, ideological ideas such as monetarism were advocated by her devoted supporters like Sir Keith Joseph,[178] but she was equally careful to listen to those few more liberal grandees who loyally participated in her success – Peter Carrington[179] and William Whitelaw[180] to name the most significant.

She attracted the "lunatic right" at home and abroad but was never one of them. When she used the often quoted expression "one of us", I think she was referring to those who put "cause" before party and honour and individual freedom before bureaucracy. Totalitarianism in all its forms was the enemy, hence her Euroscepticism.

At 5 p.m. on November 15 1989, I ascended the famous staircase at 10 Downing Street, accompanying the former President Jayewardene[181] of Sri Lanka for tea with Prime Minister Thatcher. The President had been very disappointed not to have had a state visit to the UK[182] and had asked whether I could arrange an informal visit following his retirement.

It was a great pleasure to organize this, as each suggestion of a meeting or event was most enthusiastically received. The Prime Minister was no exception, and I was informed that she would be sure to leave

---

178 Keith Sinjohn Joseph, Baron Joseph (1918–94) was a British barrister and politician.
179 Peter Alexander Rupert Carrington, 6th Baron Carrington (born 1919), a British Conservative politician.
180 William Stephen Ian Whitelaw, 1st Viscount Whitelaw (1918–99) was a British Conservative Party politician.
181 Junius Richard Jayewardene (1906–1996) was the first Executive President of Sri Lanka, serving from 1978 till 1989. See chapter 18
182 Due to a UK general election and his own Tamil uprising in 1983.

Prime Minister's Questions in the House of Commons early if necessary to promptly receive J.R.

A warm welcome was extended by the Prime Minister as we entered into the first-floor drawing room, and tea was instantly served. Charles Powell[183] was on hand to take notes.

"It is *so* good to see you, Mr President. I will *never* forget that you were the *very* first to ring me, at 6 o'clock, on the morning of our Falklands initiative. What encouragement. But, may I ask you, why?"

"Well, Prime Minister, I have *every* confidence in you and hoped that after you had put the Argentinians in their place, you would send your fleet to protect *me* from the Indians!"

The Prime Minister had heard everything before and did not bat an eye.

"Michael, thank you for bringing this *great* man, and don't hesitate to bring others." Thus ended an hour's fascinating discussion.

I remembered her words, and I did! Four years later, I made my second introduction. It was Prime Minister Samadov[184] of Tajikistan – a rather different character to J.R.

Margaret Thatcher had given every encouragement to a small group of us to put together an aviation company called Tajik Air. It was led by aviation expert Bahman Daneshmand. The government of Tajikistan had authorized us to create for them an international airline, pledging fifty per cent financial support as shareholders.

My responsibility was to organize an air treaty between Tajikistan and the UK and to obtain a slot at Heathrow – rather an audacious move for a fledgling airline – whilst Bahman organized the lease of the first plane (a Boeing 747) and established a sales operation.

All was in place by November 1994. Meanwhile, it was important for the Prime Minister of Tajikistan to meet the Prime Minister of the United Kingdom. Thus on the 7 March 1994, a dinner was held at Grosvenor House, Park Lane, the only problem being that Prime

---

183 Charles David Powell, Baron Powell of Bayswater (born 1941), a diplomat, politician, and businessman. He served as a key foreign policy advisor to British Prime Minister Margaret Thatcher during the 1980s.
184 Abdujalil Akhadovich Samadov (1949–2004) was prime minister of Tajikistan between December 18 1993 and December 2 1994.

Minister Samadov could not speak English and Prime Minister Thatcher could not speak Russian!

I rang Marina Galitzine, daughter of Princess Valentine Galitzine, who was fascinated to act as interpreter between one whose family was associated with the murder of her ancestors and one who had encouraged perestroika! I suggested she might feel free to use a little poetic license during her lengthy interpretations.

Despite minor diplomatic difficulties, *Snow Leopard* made her historic maiden flight that November – the first jumbo jet ever to fly into central Asia.[185]

In October 2008, Jaanus Reiser[186] asked me if I could introduce his prime minister, Mart Laar,[187] to Margaret Thatcher, something that Conservative Central Office had failed to do. I made the arrangement through the ever helpful Mary Wakeley,[188] and the visit took place on 3 November at Chesham Place. I had warned the Estonian Prime Minister that Lady Thatcher[189] was no fan of the European Union and would undoubtedly raise the issue. Upon our arrival, the Iron Lady welcomed Mart Laar, first turning to me:

"First you brought President Jayewardene, next Prime Minister Samadov, and now Prime Minister Laar – and he is one of us – but why [turning to Laar] did you leave one union for another?"

Laar was not slow in his response. "For the money, Lady Thatcher."

Mart Laar went on to write a book, *Estonia: Little Country that Could*, and I was asked to get the Thatchers to attend its London launch. It was an interesting evening. I had been rung up by Eyhab Jumean, who asked me if he could bring Saif Gaddafi[190] along to the party. I said that as long as he did not arrive with too many bodyguards, he would be welcomed. Saif brought with him a copy of *The Downing Street Years*.[191]

---

185 See www.tajikair.com
186 Estonian landowner
187 Mart Laar (born 1960) an Estonian politician. He was the prime minister of Estonia from 1992 to 1994 and from 1999 to 2002.
188 Personal assistant to Margaret Thatcher.
189 Margaret Thatcher became Lady Thatcher in 1992.
190 Saif al-Islam Muammar al-Gaddafi (born 1972), a son of Muammar al-Gaddafi, leader of Libya.
191 *The Downing Street Years* by Margaret Thatcher, first published in 1993.

Approaching Lady Thatcher, he politely asked her if she would mind autographing the book.

"Of course, what is your name?"

"Gaddafi, Ma'am".

Showing not the slightest negative reaction, Lady Thatcher turned to me and said, "You can learn something from everyone". This book eventually found its way into Colonel Gaddafi's remarkable library in Tripoli, where I was shown it on my visit to Libya in September 2005.

As the evening continued, Margaret Thatcher invited Mart Laar to make a speech about his book. After a few minutes the speech was interrupted by a loud voice.

"Is he speaking in Russian?"

"No, in Estonian!"

The penetrating eyes of the Iron Lady spotted the two offenders, and she marched towards them, handbag aloft.

"Denis, shut up! The Prime Minister of *Estonia* is speaking."

Both Sir Denis[192] and Sir David[193] were silenced. The Russian-Estonian theme continued over dinner, at which last-minute changes to the table plan meant I had to place Vera Protasova[194] exactly opposite Lady Thatcher. At once the two "clicked".

"Oh, I so loved my time in Russia," declared Lady Thatcher. "Such wonderful people especially that fellow Gorbachev."[195]

At this point the very diplomatic (and now sadly and greatly missed) Michael Richardson,[196] sitting on Lady Thatcher's left, whispered to her that the Prime Minister of Estonia was on her right and that he was not the greatest fan of Russia!

---

192 Major Sir Denis Thatcher, 1st Baronet (1915–2003) was a British businessman, and the husband of the former British Prime Minister, Margaret Thatcher.
193 Sir David O'Grady Roche (born 1947), the 5th Baronet Roche of Carass, Co. Limerick in Ireland.
194 See chapter 27.
195 Mikhail Sergeyevich Gorbachev (born 1931), the seventh and last General Secretary of the Communist Party of the Soviet Union, serving from 1985 until 1991, and the last head of state of the USSR, serving from 1988 until its collapse in 1991.
196 Sir Michael Richardson (1925–2003) was a banker, financier.

Any sense of embarrassment was quickly dispelled. My eccentric American friend John Franchi had persuaded me to invite him to the dinner with his new very pregnant Romanian wife.

Sir Denis, greatly fascinated by this, called over the table to Sir Michael. "You know, old boy, she is just about to drop that child right in the middle of dinner."

"Yes," responded Sir Michael. "Doesn't she closely resemble that lovely thing we met …?"

"Shut up," Denis interrupted him. "Margaret doesn't know about her."

Somehow that dinner ended on a happy note, but if only my table could have talked what further secrets would it have revealed?

Sadly, Sir Denis died on 26 June 2003, and life for Margaret Thatcher would never be the same again.

I called on her several times afterwards – usually to get her to autograph a book of hers for a friend. Once I called[197] to get a book signed for an Estonian acquaintance[198] who had kindly invited me to his wedding. He was a very rich man who had everything – except a book signed by Lady Thatcher.

"How many times has he been married?" enquired the great lady, hesitating before inscribing the book.

"Well, at least once before."

"Don't you think you had better find out before I sign?"

It took a little gentle persuasion to get her to sign just before I leapt with great relief into a taxi for the airport to get to the wedding on time!

---

197 In December 2002
198 Hans H. Luik (born 1961) a journalist and businessman.

23: Maryam Rajavi

"*In all probability she is* the most threatened woman in the world," declared the Swedish news magazine *Expressen* in 1994. By 1996 the London *Times* listed her as "one of the most powerful woman in the world".

Yet few in Britain had heard of her when I was asked to introduce her in that same year.

It happened like this. On January 14 1995, I was asked to receive a "top secret" delegation in my London office. It was a Saturday morning, so no staff were present to witness the strange assembly of eight unidentified Iranians. I agreed to the meeting only because I was greatly encouraged to do so by a close Iranian friend. He did not wish to appear or indeed thereafter be associated with the proceedings.

My visitors turned out to be leaders of the People's Mujahedin Organization of Iran (PMOI). Their purpose was to enlist my support in getting their founder, Maryam Rajavi, into the UK to meet potential significant supporters. It was explained that Mrs Rajavi was also president-elect of the National Council of Resistance of Iran. There were a couple of problems to overcome. First, the PMOI was generally regarded as a terrorist organization, and second, anyone assisting them would be on the Iranian mullahs' hit list.

I listened to the delegation's presentation and arguments for several hours, becoming more and more convinced of the legitimacy of their cause. At the end of the meeting, I agreed to consider their request and to report back to a secret address in London in due course.

Over the next few weeks, I carefully researched the background and history of the PMOI, the National Council of Resistance of Iran

(NCRI), Maryam Rajavi, and her more notorious husband Massoud Rajavi.[199]

Massoud had opposed the Shah's[200] government since his student days. He was an enthusiastic supporter of the revolution[201] but soon clashed with Ayatollah Khomeini's[202] regime over the suppression of liberties. In 1981 he fled to Paris, having narrowly escaped execution, and thence on to Iraq at the invitation of Saddam Hussein.[203] With Hussein's assistance, he founded the PMOI in 1985 with Maryam, his wife, as cofounder.

Massoud was to develop the military side of the resistance movement from its HQ at Camp Ashraf, conveniently situated 120 kilometres west of the Iranian border and 60 kilometres north of Baghdad. Maryam was to develop the political wing from the French HQ at Auvers-sur-Oise, the well-known Paris suburb.

In 1993 she was elected president-elect of the National Council of Resistance of Iran (NCRI), an umbrella coalition of which the PMOI is the primary member organization. An important aspect of Mrs Rajavi's policy is that women should have equal rights with men in social and political activities. To this, the ayatollahs have not taken kindly.

Having decided to assist Mrs Rajavi, after several more clandestine meetings in London, I enlisted the support of Sir William Shelton[204]

---

199 Massoud Rajavi (born 1948) the President of the National Council of Resistance of Iran and the leader of People's Mujahedin of Iran (PMOI, also known as the MEK), an opposition organization active inside and outside of Iran.
200 Mohammad Rezā Shāh Pahlavi, Shah of Iran, (1919–1980) was the Shah of Iran from 16 September 1941 until his overthrow by the Iranian Revolution on 11 February 1979.
201 The Islamic Revolution (also known as the Iranian Revolution or 1979 Revolution) refers to events involving the overthrow of Iran's monarchy (Pahlavi dynasty) under Shah Mohammad Reza Pahlavi and its replacement with an Islamic republic under Ayatollah Ruhollah Khomeini, the leader of the revolution.
202 Syed Ruhollah Moosavi Khomeini (1900–1989) was an Iranian religious leader and politician and leader of the 1979 Iranian Revolution which saw the overthrow of Mohammad Reza Pahlavi, the Shah of Iran.
203 Saddam Hussein Abd al-Majid al-Tikriti (1937–2006) was the President of Iraq from 16 July 1979 until 9 April 2003.
204 Sir William Jeremy Masefield Shelton, known as Bill Shelton (1929–2003) was a Conservative Party politician in the United Kingdom, former Parliamentary Private Secretary to Margaret Thatcher.

and Jonathan Guinness,[205] both experienced and well-connected in the political world. An early priority was to meet Maryam Rajavi, and on 6 September 1995 we three took an early train to Paris and then on by taxi to Auvers-sur-Oise.

Expected, we were quickly taken through heavy security into a reception room and given tea. A few minutes later several women appeared, but there was no doubt as to which was the leader.

Since that first meeting, I have been privileged to meet Maryam Rajavi several times in contrasting circumstances. On all occasions she has maintained a quiet, calm, almost serene, but very strong presence. She is a natural leader because she inspires confidence consistently, whether in private conversation, conducting a meeting, or addressing tens of thousands of supporters.

We spent three hours discussing the possibilities of a UK visit, including a delicious lunch, before heading back to London with much to think about and much to do.

Clearly the mullahs' propaganda machine had been most effective in convincing western governments to have nothing to do with these "terrorists". Not only did I find that the NCRI and PMOI were strongly opposed by the Tehran regime who, ironically, had influenced most of the so-called democratic world against them, but also by many Iranians who viewed them with deep suspicion.

In other words, all the progress made by the Rajavis has been against very high odds. But progress, very slow, and very sure there has been – a huge lesson in perseverance!

Maryam Rajavi already had a few influential supporters in London, notably Lord Avebury.[206] and I met him a few days after the Paris adventure. He was very supportive but also realistically doubtful about the prospects for a successful visit – or even any visit at all. For instance, we faced the simple matter of how to obtain a visa.

Suffice it to say that a visa was obtained on medical grounds, plans were well and truly made, and Mrs Rajavi arrived in London with a thirty-strong entourage in June 1996.

---

205 See chapter 13.
206 Eric Reginald Lubbock, 4th Baron Avebury, PC (born 1928) an English politician.

It was difficult enough to encourage prominent and influential people to meet Mrs Rajavi; due to the negative propaganda, this was no easy task. For example, first Margaret Thatcher enthusiastically accepted and then at the last minute declined, and the Archbishop of Canterbury and the Cardinal of Westminster did likewise. On top of this, there was the question of security and, of course, the Foreign Office.

In November 1995 I had approached Nick Brown, then head of the Middle East Department of the Foreign Office, to gauge his reaction to Maryam Rajavi. I followed this first meeting by sending him a series of press cuttings about her recent visit to Norway. Despite his misgivings, I felt Nick warming to the idea of a possible visit to London, but strictly on a low-key private basis. This was not at all what we had planned, but I decided to go along with it for the time being.

By April 1996, Mrs Rajavi decided to proceed with the visit despite an incomplete programme.

My next task was to notify the police, who under the supervision of Superintendent Frank Armstrong became extremely helpful both in the pre-planning stage and most discreetly throughout the visit.

Further discussions took place with Nick Brown, who suspected that there was much more to the visit than medical matters; he once said that the involvement of Lord Avebury was "too coincidental".

I don't think it was too much of a surprise to Nick when on 5 June I raised the subject of "The Concert". For many months, a gala concert featuring Marzieh,[207] known as the Nightingale of Persia, had been planned, and Mrs Rajavi had realized that this would provide an excellent opportunity to make her own first public appearance in London. Officially, the event was to celebrate the fifteenth anniversary of 20 June 1981, the beginning of the Iranian people's resistance against the mullahs' regime.

On 19 June, I was asked to meet Nick Brown urgently at the Foreign Office. He said he was alarmed to hear that many thousands of Iranians were expected to attend the forthcoming event, and could I assure him that if Mrs Rajavi was present, she would not make a speech. I responded by saying that she would attend and that the audience would demand she address them and that it would be very bad if they

---

207 Marzieh (1926–2010) was a diva of Persian music.

were told the Foreign Office had forbidden the speech. I said that I felt sure Mrs Rajavi would agree to have her speech privately vetted by the Foreign Office. Nick stressed that any speech should avoid reference to the Liberation Army and should certainly not call for the overthrow of the mullahs' regime.

I hastened from the Foreign Office to Mrs Rajavi's suite at Grosvenor House, where I began my report of the Foreign Office meeting by stressing their concern about her safety. Nick had stressed "very great danger to Mrs Rajavi, her entourage, and British associates"!

I then ventured to repeat the Foreign Office's wish that she would attend the event, but should not speak: this would be a very positive sign to HM's Government. "If this is achieved a dialogue can be established aimed at persuading HM's Government that the NCRI *is* a suitable alternative.[208]"

Mrs Rajavi was thoughtful and then said, "I understand the Foreign Office position but cannot let the people down. You know how to put this over diplomatically."

I met Nick again the following morning with the report that Mrs Rajavi felt she had no alternative but to give a speech; that it would be moderate with no reference to the overthrow of the regime or the Resistance Army. I also stressed that she had agreed to no media coverage within the UK.

In the event, London's Earl's Court was the scene of the biggest ever gathering of Iranians outside Iran, as 25,000 people from all over the world gathered to hear Mrs Rajavi's speech, the final very moderate and inspiring title of which was "Women, voice of the oppressed". She spoke of the Iranian struggle with gender-based oppression, the necessity of forming a united anti-fundamentalist front, and the rights of women in a future democratic Iran.

The atmosphere was electric, and the ecstatic multitude roared their approval, repeatedly interrupting the speech to endorse her plans of action. The ovation lasted twenty minutes. Mrs Rajavi had revealed her Churchill-like powers, and Lord Avebury sat quietly beside her.

---

208 Private record of the meeting, 19 June 1996.

Despite the unenthusiastic reception on the part of the British establishment, the Earl's Court event alone more than justified Mrs Rajavi's visit to London.

Typical of all truly great personalities, Mrs Rajavi does not forget any detail of protocol, good manners or kindness. On the evening of 8 August, a beautiful Persian carpet was delivered to my Kensington apartment with a simple note:

Thank you with all my heart for your advice and guidance,

Maryam Rajavi

I responded thus:

8th August 1996

My dear Mrs Rajavi,

I cannot thank you enough for the kind thought, typical of you, in sending me the lovely Persian carpet. It will always remind me of a brave, generous, gracious, and lovely lady.

I do hope you feel you are returning to France from a truly worthwhile visit in London – especially the memorable gathering in Earl's Court. My greatest regret is that we were unable to arrange the meeting with Lady Thatcher – this time. She has been somewhat influenced by a sceptical element in the Foreign Office where we still have much work of education to do. I know as a great leader you do not underestimate the opposition!

I am delighted to hear that your health is now excellent and greatly look forward to meeting you again in Paris!

Warmest regards,

Michael

Following the American invasion of Iraq in 2003, Massoud Rajavi disappeared, assumed dead, since when Maryam Rajavi has assumed all leadership responsibilities of the NCRI and PMOI.

Next stop – Iran?

24: Jim Davidson

Jim Davidson, OBE

*I*t was Bill Shelton[209] who, one fine morning in September 1996, proposed that he introduce me to Jim. We had been discussing the National Lottery[210] and the kinds of projects it might support. Bill had recently met Jim Davidson, who had asked his advice about possible lottery support for the restoration of Wellington Pier, Great Yarmouth in Norfolk. Knowing of my Norfolk connections, Bill had decided to consult me. Rather more interested in meeting Jim than in Wellington Pier, I enthusiastically agreed to meet the famous star of stage and screen.

Thus a few days later, Bill hosted a lunch at the Carlton Club, and I came face to face with the great man.

Until then Jim had been known to me as an entertaining comedian who was never afraid of hard verbal punches, often below the belt, and gloriously *apolitically* correct! The king of *The Generation Game*,[211] though ever amusing and just as entertaining in private as in public, now revealed a serious side of his character.

I got to know right away Jim the philanthropist. As I was to discover over the coming years, Jim's philanthropy is genuine, heartfelt, and

---

209 Sir William Jeremy Masefield Shelton, commonly known as Bill Shelton (1929–2003) was a Conservative Party politician in the United Kingdom.
210 The National Lottery was set up in 1993, and is regulated by the National Lottery Commission.
211 *The Generation Game* was a British game show produced by the BBC in which four teams of two (people from the same family, but different generations, hence the title of the show) competed to win prizes. The programme was first broadcast in 1971 under the title *Bruce Forsyth and the Generation Game* and ran until 1982, and again from 1990 until 2002.

often spontaneous even sometimes to his own detriment. When he cares about something, all other considerations become secondary.

Over a hearty lunch we got down to business, and it was agreed that Bill and I should do our best to put together an appropriate application for lottery funding for the pier.

This was rather vital for Jim, as he had already committed over £750,000 of his own money to restore the historic Winter Garden within the pier complex and to create a centre of entertainment. Despite Bill's political experience and (dare I say?) connections and my own "literary expertise", our application sadly failed. Naturally, this did not deter Jim, who continued with the project, making frequent appearances to the delight of the local population. In fact, Jim admitted to me that he is really a Norfolk man at heart and is indeed a particular friend of the Norfolk lifeboat men[212] to this day. Patriotism rather than economics had prevailed.

And it is patriotism that is a main theme of Jim's life.

In April of 1998 he rang me to say, "I have been deeply concerned about the lack of live entertainment for our troops deployed around the world and have decided to set up an organization called the British Forces Foundation. Please, help me."

Mostly because it was from Jim, it was a request I could not refuse!

At that time British troops were serving in over thirty countries, and Jim's aim was to boost their morale with live shows and visits from celebrities and sports stars. He had been entertaining troops since 1974, when "the old shows used to cost four pence to put on, but now a massive amount is involved. The armed forces are there to defend our country and make us all feel great. I think it is our duty to make *them* all feel great.[213]" This was Jim's mantra and provided the ethos of the organization.

I met with Jim to discuss the setting up of the organization which clearly depended for its success on both recognition and cash. Jim asked me to enlist the support of "appropriate names", including Margaret Thatcher.

---

212 Jim had spent happy holidays as a child in the Norfolk Broads.
213 *The Sun*, April 9 1999.

Luckily, I had recently met Rex Hunt,[214] of whom Margaret Thatcher was a great admirer. Rex agreed at once and enlisted the support of Vera Lynn.[215] Meanwhile, Jim had brought in Harry Secombe,[216] and by September it was time to approach Margaret Thatcher from a position of strength. Of course, she agreed with enthusiasm and on 22 September became patron of the British Forces Foundation.

By 1999 Admiral Sir Jock Slater,[217] General Arthur Denaro,[218] Air Vice Marshal David Crwys-Williams,[219] and Laurie Mansfield, the chairman of International Artists, had become founder trustees and, to quote Jim, "The show was truly on the road."

Fundraising was a top priority, and in February it was decided to establish an inaugural ball committee headed by HRH Princess Katarina of Yugoslavia,[220] a leading member of London society.

Katarina enthused a group of well-connected Londoners to plan the ball scheduled for 25 May. In March Sir Donald Gosling[221] donated the first significant sum of £20,000, and under Jim's charismatic leadership, confidence was high.

Princess Katarina was placed in an impossible position when NATO Forces began their bombardment of Yugoslavia on 24 March and shortly afterwards had to resign from the leadership of the committee. Jim asked me to stand in as chairman of the ball committee, and only then did I understand the very hard work entailed!

---

214 Sir Rex Masterman Hunt (born 1926) a British diplomat and colonial administrator. He was Governor, Commander-in-Chief, and Vice Admiral of the Falkland Islands between 1980 and September 1985.
215 Dame Vera Lynn, or Vera Margaret Welch (born 1917) an English singer and actress whose musical recordings and performances were enormously popular during World War II.
216 Sir Harry Donald Secombe (1921–2001) was a Welsh entertainer with a talent for comedy and a noted fine tenor singing voice.
217 Admiral Sir John Cunningham Kirkwood Slater (born 1938) served as First Sea Lord and Chief of the Naval Staff. He was equerry to HM the Queen from 1968 to 1971.
218 Major General Arthur Denaro, CBE (born 1948), a senior figure within the British Army. Former Commandant, Royal Military Academy, Sandhurst.
219 Air Vice Marshal David Crwys-William (born 1940) was Commander British Forces Falkland Islands from August 1988 to August 1989.
220 See chapter 14
221 Sir Donald Gosling (born 1929)

The British Forces Foundation was officially launched on 6 May. With great aplomb, Jim arrived with the Royal Marines on board one of their high speed, rigid, inflatable boats at *HMS President*, where he was joined by his fellow trustees and servicemen from all three armed services, serenaded by the popular band Girl Nation. He had just returned from a four-day visit entertaining the troops in Macedonia, which he said had boosted his energy and enthusiasm:

> When young soldiers, sailors and airmen are a long way from home, doing their bit for their country, they like to know that people care back here. The appearance of a well-known entertainer helps give them that reassurance – as well as cheering them up, I hope!

The ball followed on 25 May, and it could hardly fail to succeed with the heady combination of Margaret Thatcher and the Spice Girls! It raised over £60,000.

On 29 October, Arthur Denaro hosted a luncheon for the foundation at Sandhurst, honoured by the presence of Prince Charles. I took several friends along, including Dr Abdulaziz Ali Al-Quaiti, descendent of the sultans of Hadhramaut, Yemen. Dr Al Quaiti fascinated Prince Charles by telling him of his purchase of the Humber car used by Her Majesty the Queen on her visit to Yemen in 1954. He presented the Prince with a copy of his book *Sultan Ali bin Salah al-Quaiti: Half a Century of Political Struggle in Hadhramaut*, which I'm sure HRH read with relish.

Other entertaining characters present included Sir Harry Secombe[222] and Sir Jimmy Savile.[223] As soon as Prince Charles left at 3 p.m., we lit up our cigars!

It was not long afterwards that His Royal Highness agreed to become patron, Margaret Thatcher most graciously agreeing to step down into the role of president. Since then under the direction of Mark

---

222 Sir Harry Donald Secombe CBE (1921–2001) was a Welsh entertainer.
223 Sir James Wilson Vincent Savile OBE, KCSG (born 1926) an English DJ, actor and media personality.

Cann[224] the foundation has gone on from strength to strength to play a major role in caring for the wellbeing of the British Forces.

Jim, like most of us, has had his ups and downs, the downs being mostly financial. Throughout, his real friends, including Prince Charles, have stood solidly behind him and today he has re-emerged stronger than ever to the delight of his friends and fans alike.

A true comedian has a very realistic understanding of life. Hence there is a well-known narrow line between comedy and tragedy. Jim has known the depths as well as the heights. One evening I was interrupted during dinner in a friend's house by the butler who whispered in my ear, "Please go at once, Sir, to Annabel's. Your friend Jim is distressed."

I excused myself from the table and hastened to the club to be greeted by Ted,[225] "Jim is sitting alone by the fire and will not speak to anyone."

I approached Jim, who smiled through an alcoholic haze, "Good to see you, old chap. I needed to see you to be cheered up!"

I was delighted to be there when needed. One morning Jim had rung me, as if by telepathy, just as I had heard some bad news about someone very close. Without hesitation he sprang into action and provided enormous and extremely inspiring assistance, even to the extent of delaying a TV rehearsal. He had proved himself to be the best of men and truest of friends.

I rang Jim the other day just for old times' sake and to tell him of his inclusion in this book! Touching on the subject of Annabel's, he said, "The best moment was when you tried to demonstrate the dagger dance on a table.[226] It did not go down too well with the *maitre d'* as a few glasses and plates went flying – happy days!"

---

224 Major Mark Cann (born 1965) the Chief Executive of the British Forces Foundation and its trading company, Forces Events Ltd.
225 Ted Racki, famous head doorman at *Annabel's* for forty years.
226 This I had first witnessed at the Waldorf Astoria Hotel danced successfully by Prince Sergei Obolensky in 1966.

25: Shafik Jumean

General Ayman Shafik Jumean

Jordanians and Britons have enjoyed cordial relations since the inception of the Kingdom – and this despite the machinations of politicians. Nor is it just a mesmeric fascination that attracts the romantically inclined British Arabist to the Middle East in general. Jordan in particular holds a special place in the British heart. Education, both civil and military, has played a significant role. So many Jordanians have attended British schools and universities, and Sandhurst[227] has produced a large number of officers for the Royal Jordanian Army. English is spoken extensively – usually very well enunciated and articulated – amongst the professional classes. And to cap it all, the King has an English mother.

The Jordanian Bedouin instinctively comprehends British social norms because the old desert chivalry is very close to the traditional conduct of a gentleman!

General Shafik Jumean moved effortlessly between his Jordanian and British life. Of distinguished appearance, he had a military bearing and gentle manner that disguised a tough determination. He was the epitome of a Jordanian British officer.

On the 5 July 1999, a thousand people attended the London memorial service for perhaps the greatest of all Jordanians – His Majesty King Hussein bin Talal.

Today we hear a lot of nonsense about the incompatibility of Christianity and Islam. (As I write, an American lunatic is proposing to publically burn copies of the Koran.) King Hussein was a direct

---

[227] The Royal Military Academy Sandhurst (RMAS), commonly known as Sandhurst, is the British Army officer training centre.

descendent of Mohammed[228] and a fervent Muslim. Yet he was brought up at school in England[229] within a Christian atmosphere and was as familiar with the Psalms of David as any Christian – or Jew for that matter.

Thus, in the great cathedral church of St Paul's, Christian hymns and anthems, prayers, and Gospel mingled with a reading from the Qur'an read by the half-English newly appointed King Abdullah. Perhaps the highlight of the services was a moving address given by Prince Charles that included the memorable words, "A man amongst men, a king amongst kings."

Inspired by the service, I decided to have a quiet and reflective lunch and adjourned to the Clermont Club, where I expected to be undisturbed. Sitting down at my table I saw just one other – General Shafik. We joined forces, and he told me he had had the same idea – to contemplate on the amazing event we had both been privileged to witness.

I had met the General from time to time in the past but it was on this occasion that I got to know him and to warm to his personality.

Major General Shafik Jumean,[230] born in Amman, had attended Sandhurst in 1950, after which he was commissioned in the Royal Jordanian Armed Forces, where he was assigned as operations officer in the Artillery Headquarters. He rose rapidly through the ranks – battery commander, Artillery; executive officer, Infantry Brigade; commander, Artillery Regiment – until by 1960 he had become deputy commander of the Royal Jordanian Air Forces.

As we shall see, the Jumean family has marched closely with the Hashemite royal family since the inception of the Kingdom, and it was therefore not surprising that in 1961 Shafik became personal aide to King Hussein.

---

[228] Mohammad ibn 'Abdullāh (ca. 570/571–632) was the founder of the religion of Islam and is regarded by Muslims as a messenger and prophet of God (*Allāh*), the greatest law-bearer in a series of Islamic prophets and by most Muslims the last prophet as taught by the Qur'an.
[229] Harrow school
[230] General Shafik Jumean (1928–2001)

If My Table Could Talk

For the next ten years, he had an extremely busy and interesting life that involved adventures in both Lebanon and Greece, which he loved to relate to me over a stiff whisky in one of his several London clubs.

From 1973 to 1978, Shafik was given the huge responsibility of being Defence and Armed Forces Attaché in Washington D.C. He was soon appointed Dean of the Association of Military Attaches, which included over 300 officers as members from around the world. It was during this period that he had another, perhaps even bigger, responsibility – that of looking after HRH Prince Abdullah. Some strange fate had led King Hussein to entrust his son, who was not expected at that time to become the future king, to the personal supervision of Shafik and the loving care of his family.

Over the Clermont luncheon, Shafik told me of his more recent experiences in the commercial world. He had become chairman of several businesses, ranging from publishing to electronics. One of his more recent ventures, however, was in tourism, and when he heard of my recent appointment as chairman of the Guild of Travel & Tourism, we decided to meet again in the near future.

Sure enough, just a few days later, Shafik telephoned me and invited me to lunch, again at the Clermont, and informed me that we would be joined by HRH Prince Mohammed.

From 1978 until 1982, Shafik had been chief of staff to His Royal Highness, and during this time they had established a deep and abiding friendship. The morning before our lunch, they had been visiting bookshops searching for works on Napoleon, about whom Prince Mohammed is an expert. They had failed to find Alistair Horne's[231] recently published biography, but by good fortune I had two copies and offered one to the prince. He accepted and in return invited me to visit his private library on my next visit to Amman.

"You are very privileged," said Shafik. "You will be the only Englishman to have visited his private collection."

I arrived in Jordan on October 20 2000 after an absence of several years. Despite the late hour, Shafik was at the airport with Abdulla, his driver and former batman of over thirty years.

---

231 Sir Alistair Allan Horne (born 1925)

"Tomorrow," he said, "I will take you to see my birthplace, and you will then understand more about me and my family."

Next morning we set off to Madaba, some twenty miles south of Amman. It is ancient and steeped in Jewish, Christian, and Muslim history. Christianity has been established since its earliest days, and Shafik took me first to see the Greek Orthodox Basilica of St George, wherein is the amazing and famous mosaic map of the sixth century, depicting hills and valleys, villages and towns in Palestine and the Nile Delta. Shafik's own family have been Orthodox Christians for many centuries, in common with many of the oldest Bedouin families of this area.

From the church we went to the old quarter, which is Shafik's birthplace. He led me up an ancient wooden staircase into a small room.

"This is where I was born. But more important, this is where my grandfather sat with King Abdullah I bin al-Hussein[232] in 1946. You see Muslim and Christian blended together to form the ethos of this kingdom, which is tolerance and cooperation."

Yes, I had begun to understand more about Shafik, his family, and his country.

We had a nourishing mezé and a glass of local wine before journeying back to Amman for my second interesting engagement of the day – the visit to Prince Mohammed's palace.

The palace had been recently built – grand, classical, and impressive, as befitted the residence of the brother of the King.

"It even makes a great impression on the Saudi royal visitors," said Shafik with a wink.

Recognizing the General, the security guards admitted us at once into a small ante-room by the main entrance to find Prince Mohammed already waiting for us. Fortunately, I had taken my camera and was given permission to record the event. Our host led us, rather too quickly, round the state rooms, and it was not possible to take in their clearly fascinating contents. Before I knew it, we were inside a lift, rising up several floors before stepping into a dimly lit corridor.

---

[232] Abdullah I bin al-Hussein, King of Jordan (1882–1951) born in Mecca, Ottoman Empire, (in modern-day Saudi Arabia).

"Here we are," said the Prince, leading us towards a main doorway. "This is my *sanctum sanctorum*."

The room is massive, containing on one side a huge library and, of course, the collection of Napoleonic books.

Tea was served and interesting books proudly shown. Then I noticed a life-size cut-out figure of John Wayne.[233] "Another of my hero's," explained my charming host, who never ceased to astonish me.

I was not surprised to see another wonder – a life-size chess set! Out of earshot of His Royal Highness, Shafik muttered, "Do not challenge him to a game. It will last for hours, and he must always win!"

Probably our host did hear because he said, with a smile, "Perhaps you would prefer to try out my exercise bike?" I politely refused his kind offer, asking him instead to comment on some of the many framed certificates and photographs scattered around the room.

There are few things more interesting than to visit the private quarters of a public person, and this visit was no exception. Indeed, it brought home to me the deep humanity of a quiet, unassuming, and remarkable man who had for years been caught up in the dramatic and fast development of his country, a very steady and solid support for his brother.

On the fast track from Jordan, Shafik and I were headed for Estonia. In common with most generals, Shafik could not accept retirement. He wanted constant occupation and responsibility. Having had some experience of diplomatic work[234] and knowing of my connections in Estonia, Shafik suggested that he would be the best person to be its honorary consul in Jordan.

Meetings were held in the Estonian Foreign Ministry, at which it was explained that diplomatic relations must first be established between the two countries. Several weeks later and after frequent and frantic telephone calls, the royal decree was issued on 15 November to which the official Estonian response was as follows:

---

233 Marion Mitchell Morrison (1907–79), better known by his stage name John Wayne, was an Academy Award-winning American film actor, director, and producer.
234 He had held the position of honorary consul for the Philippines.

The Ministry of Foreign Affairs of the Republic of Estonia presents its compliments to the Ministry of Foreign Affairs of the Hashemite Kingdom of Jordan, and has the honour to inform the Ministry that the Estonian Government wishes to request the consent of the Government of Jordan to establish an Honorary Consulate General in Amman, Jordan, to be headed by an Estonian Honorary Consul General and which will be housed in the Villa located between the Swiss Embassy and the South Korean Embassy.

In this connection the Estonian Government is nominating General (Ret.) Shafik Jumean a distinguished citizen of Jordan, as Honorary Consul General of Estonia in Amman. Enclosed is the Curriculum Vitae of General Jumean and copy of the recommendation of HRH Prince Mohammed.

If the Government of the Hashemite Kingdom of Jordan agrees to the opening of an Estonian Honorary Consulate General in Amman it would be highly appreciated if the exequatur of General Shafik Jumean be immediately issued so that there will be no delay in the consular representation of the Estonian Government in Jordan.

Shafik remained the very affective honorary consul until his death when, by pre-arrangement made during his final visit to Tallinn in October 2003, his son Ayman took over the responsibilities.

This final visit had been planned for some time in coordination with both of his sons, Ayman, and Eyhab, who provided the private jet and made the accommodation arrangements.

The visit partly coincided with the state visit of Patriarch Alexy II.[235] Eyhab particularly wanted to visit Alexander Nevsky Cathedral during a quiet period to light a candle for his mother. This was difficult amidst the excited crowds. We succeeded, and he also found her an appropriate icon.

---

235 H.H. Patriarch Alexy II (1929–2008) was the 15th Patriarch of Moscow and All Russia, the primate of the Russian Orthodox Church.

Over the next few years, Shafik and I met mostly in London, which was truly his second home. There he combined entertainment for Prince Mohammed, business meetings, and diplomatic initiatives for Estonia with regular relaxation at the Clermont.

Otherwise we spoke regularly on the telephone. One day I rang his office to hear a voice saying, "Unfortunately the General has died." I detected a familiar sound in the voice! He had not lost his sense of humour.

He actually died in London on 25 August 2007. His driver Abdulla told me how he arrived at Albert Hall Gardens to find his boss peacefully sleeping on the floor. Meeting me recently at Amman airport, Abdulla said, "Sir, I had the privilege of serving your friend, a perfect gentleman".

Later I was accompanied by Ayman to visit Metropolitan Benedictus at the Greek Orthodox Cathedral in Amman. This was where Shafik had spent many reflective hours during his very active life.

"A man of wisdom," said the Archbishop. Indeed, I thought.

26: Summer

Summer Watson

One glorious *summer's evening* in 2000 I attended a sumptuous banquet at Spencer House[236] with Yvonne Bristol.[237] Our host was HRH Prince Andrew, and we were favoured by the inspiring voice of Kiri Te Kanawa.[238]

I was a very lucky man, for not only did I have the charming Yvonne, a friend of many years, on my right but a beautiful younger woman on my left. She introduced herself as Summer.[239]

I thought it an appropriate name for a lovely girl on a perfect summer's night! She told me something of her life and her aspiration to be an opera singer. Throughout the evening, I was aware of the watchful eye of Prince Andrew.

A few days later I received a telephone call. It was Summer. After a few minutes conversation, I invited her to dinner.

At that memorable dinner at Mark's Club, I learned more of Summer's life and challenges. Her greatest challenge was how to finance her career. Essentially, this boiled down to covering her music college fees over the next two or three years. She told me of Prince Andrew's encouragement and desire to help her. Impressed by her determination and conviction that she would become not just an opera singer, but a great one, I promised to think about how best I could help.

---

236 Spencer House, London, was built in 1756-66 for John, First Earl Spencer, an ancestor of Diana, Princess of Wales (1961–97).
237 Yvonne, Marchioness of Bristol (born 1945).
238 Dame Kiri Janette Te Kanawa (born 1944), a New Zealand soprano who has had a highly successful international opera career since 1968.
239 Summer Watson (born 1980).

A few days later came another telephone call, this time from Prince Andrew. Summer had told him of our conversation, and he was interested to know how I might assist. I asked him how much he thought would be required to cover all Summer's college fees, and he thought the sum would be about £40,000. I had an idea. I suggested that I could get some friends to subscribe a few thousand pounds each to attend a lunch or dinner with His Royal Highness.

"It will be necessary for you, Sir, to spare a few hours, say over three meals. My friends will be interested to meet you and hence subscribe."

Prince Andrew at once agreed and said that his secretary would be in touch with some available dates. I immediately rang several friends who responded enthusiastically to the proposition. One, Crispin Culbertson,[240] agreed to fly over from the United States. He is a golfer and was delighted with an opportunity to meet with Prince Andrew, who is an expert golfer. For £2,000 I said he could sit next to him. Agreed!

Next was a practical consideration. How to efficiently hold and distribute the money on Summer's behalf? She naturally did not want the responsibility of handling so large a sum. I consulted an old friend, Paul Gulbenkian,[241] who suggested we set up a trust and that he would gladly make the necessary arrangements.

Within a couple of weeks, the Summer Watson Trust was officially formed with Prince Andrew as patron and Paul and myself as trustees. Next came a suggested date for the first subscribers meal – a luncheon at Buck's Club.

It was a great success and raised about one third of the required sum. Next, we decided to hold a dinner and that more ladies should be invited, Summer having been the only lady present so far.

And what better venue could there be than Annabel's? Arrangements were duly made for December 11 2000. Ladies were invited, including Julia Belokurova.[242] Unused to meeting royalty, Julia was a little nervous.

---

240 Crispin Culbertson – US lawyer and author.
241 Paul Gulbenkian (born 1940) a lawyer, Honorary President of the Armenian Church of Saint Sarkis in London and, since 2005, chairman of the Saint Sarkis Charity Trust.
242 Julia Belokurova – *New Style* magazine.

"How shall I address His Royal Highness? What shall I do?"

"First you will courtesy and then say 'Your Royal Highness'. After that you will simply say 'Sir'."

Great joy for Prince Andrew! Upon my introducing him to Julia, she made the lowest courtesy, revealing more of her anatomy than intended whilst exclaiming "*My* Royal Highness". This set the tone for an entertaining evening, with the added benefit of more financial support for Summer.

About this time I was asked by one subscriber, "Had I ever heard Summer sing?"

I rang Prince Andrew and asked him the same question.

"Not really. Only in private. Perhaps we should hold a concert".

All, including Summer, were enthusiastic about the suggestion. A date was set, a venue decided upon,[243] and invitations sent out.

There was an excellent response, and some two hundred people gathered on January 15 2001, for Summer's debut vocal performance in the presence of Prince Andrew, her financial sponsors, and other invited guests. It was my pleasure to introduce Summer … and then we waited with bated breath!

Summer was magnificent. She appeared in a diaphanous dress, a beautiful enchantress. The pianist stuck a note – and she sang …

Yes, she *could* sing, confidently, remarkably, and memorably.

From that moment, Summer's career was made. She won the hearts and minds of all present, most of whom became her first enthusiastic fans. Summer went on quickly to sign a £1 million recording contract with Sony Classical and to emerge regularly in the UK classical charts.

A charming note came from Summer:

Dearest Michael,

As you (I am sure) are aware that I am eternally grateful for everything that you have done and continue to do so. There is simply no other word but "thank you".

---

[243] Dartmouth House, HQ of the ESU, 127 Charles St., London.

You have so much energy but so little time to spare, more the reason why I feel privileged.

I look forward to the future to see what it has in store for me.

With kind regards,

Summer

Actually this success was really due to the perception and generosity of spirit of HRH.
Perhaps another Kiri Te Kanawa had been born.

27: Vera Protasova

I spent many more hours at Vera's table than she spent at mine. In those days she lived in a spacious apartment in Mount Street at the top of three flights of stairs. Sometimes she stood at the slightly opened door waiting to greet me with a welcoming smile, which had a quickening effect upon my tiring legs as I hastened up the final steps. Most striking were Vera's eyes, glinting and twinkling with mysterious promise. The sight of these eyes made the effort of the climb a thousand times worthwhile.

I had met Vera at a Russian ball held at the Dorchester Hotel on 14 February 2002. It was at the very last minute that I was persuaded to attend by Crispin Culbertson, my American friend, who was in London for a few days recreation. (He called it cultural recreation.) Crispin was determined to attend the ball and that I should accompany him. Imagine two men going to a ball!

Dressed in white tie and tails, we found our table and I hastily looked round to see who our fellow guests were. Only one stood out. It was Vera.

She was clearly accompanied by a fellow dressed in a Hungarian hussar's uniform – only he looked neither Hungarian nor had he the distinguished air of a hussar. I wondered if he was her husband and determined at once to approach to ask his permission for his lady's hand for the first waltz. Vera intervened.

"You don't need to ask his permission. I make up my own mind – and I agree." And Vera marked her dance card accordingly.

I remember that dance very well. We simply floated round the dance floor. Vera is a good dancer. Before we returned to our table, I was clear that Vera wished to shake off her hussar, as she readily accepted my proposal to hasten to Annabel's at the first opportunity. Unfortunately, the poor fellow had left his day clothes at Vera's apartment. However, she entrusted him with a key whilst we, with Culbertson and others collected during the evening, went to the night club. I will never forget the look on the face of the now dressed-down hussar as he came into the club to deliver back the key.

"You see, he is a married man who became besotted with me," said an innocent-looking Vera, "and I do not encourage married men".

Culbertson, a happily married man, took the hint! I felt a surge of optimism.[244]

A few days later I was seated at Vera's table – perfectly round, mahogany, polished and shining, and laid up with silver, crystal, and fine napkins. Vera is a good cook, but above all she understands presentation. In 1994 at the tender age of twenty-two, she had founded a Russian restaurant in Brussels which had soon become a destination of choice among Russian food lovers in that cosmopolitan town.

This was to be the first of many lunches in Vera's apartment, for we had discovered a common theme – art.

Above all things, Vera is an artist unlimited to a single genre. She is an authority on lace – a creator and teacher from her earliest years in Moscow. She is essentially a painter in oils – evocative Russian landscapes and rather too realistic portraits. She is both a classicist and modernist, producing strange creations beyond my comprehension. And she can express herself in that most delicate of art forms, the watercolour, so beloved of the English collector.

Vera and I struck a deal. She aimed to get her master's degree in art. The only problem was that, though perfect in nearly every other way, her written English left much to be desired. At least, she imagined the examiner would think so!

Thus, whilst Vera cooked and presented delicious Russian cuisine, I interpreted her artistic insights into readable English.

These were blissful days of education – at least for me – and developing friendship. Friendship is the most important relationship it is possible to experience, and it is not so readily come by in this fast-moving world. Vera's friendship was at once spontaneous and trusting.

---

[244] I was single having been divorced in 1991.

One day, quite early on in our acquaintance, I had a sudden financial disaster. Without hesitation, Vera led me to her bank and would willingly have emptied her account of just a few hundred pounds. In fact, I needed many thousands of pounds, but it was her spontaneous gesture that mattered most.

Such was her trust that almost from the start she would lead me into her bedroom.

"Tell me which dress I should wear tonight. Close your eyes whilst I undress".

Tightly closing my eyes, I could easily visualize her beautiful form swiftly to be decked out in the chosen dress for the occasion. Lucky dress, thought I.

Vera proved hugely popular with my friends.

She made a good impression on Prince Michael.[245] This was not surprising as she is strikingly attractive, highly communicative, and P.M. enjoyed speaking to her in Russian, in which he is fluent and at ease.

A great event was our visit by helicopter to Chester Races, where P.M. was guest of honour. On the return journey, Vera cheered up the pilot by jumping into the seat next to him, very nearly taking over.

Shortly afterwards, Princess Michael invited Vera and me to luncheon at Kensington Palace. It was a glorious summer's day, so we lunched in the walled garden that had been beautifully created by the Princess following the death of Diana, Princess of Wales. As an artist with an interest in botany, Vera took a greater interest in the garden than I had expected, and I then understood a little of the keen powers of observation an accomplished artist develops.

At that time Prince and Princess Michael were showing an interest in Estonia and Estonian manor houses. It may have been this that raised the idea of Vera visiting Estonia. Whatever the reason, soon afterwards she did so.

It was July, six months after our first meeting, that Vera first visited Estonia. But this is not quite the case, for she told me of a distant memory of a visit to Tallinn from Moscow when she was a child.

---

245 HRH Prince Michael George Charles Franklin of Kent, GCVO (born 1942) a grandson of King George V and Mary of Teck.

This visit of Vera to Estonia was both joyous and disturbing. How could one not be joyful in her presence? The disturbing aspect for me was the realization that this friendship was not to be romantic!

I have already applauded friendship as the very best relationship. Yet every man knows that moment when deeper emotions stir and primeval feelings arise. And how many friendships have been devastated by this eruption?

Time and effort are needed to calm emotional storms and, reluctant though part of one was to take the time and make the effort, logic told me that Vera's friendship was the greater gift.

And we shared another bond – that of religion. Despite being born before perestroika, Vera has always had a religious belief and her very name in Russian means "faith"!

Vera's next visit to Estonia was with P.M. in March 2003 for the first royal ball in the Kadriorg Palace since the time of Nicholas II. The ball was in aid of the Children's Fire and Burn Trust, of which P.M. is patron, and Vera donated an oil painting of St Alexander's Column in Petersburg, the auction of which raised a goodly sum for the charity.

The next morning, a Sunday, P.M., Vera, Nicholas Chance, Caroline Cripps, Crispin Culbertson (who had flown over from America for this historical event), and I proceeded to St Alexander Nevsky Cathedral (my parish church when resident in Tallinn) for the Liturgy.

Said Vera later, "You have done a wonderful thing in taking P.M. to the cathedral (the first royal since Nicholas II in 1905), because this shows solid support for the local Russian Orthodox people". (These were a people who had lost the majority of their historic churches in recent years). Vera had put her finger on the pulse!

Spending more time in Estonia during the next few years, I saw less and less of Vera, but I followed her progress with interest, and a portrait she painted of me in 2002 decorated the inside flap of one of my books.[246]

She was becoming well established in London, painting the portraits of well-known characters – Tom Pendry,[247] Frederick Bristol,[248] Anthony Gurney,[249] Canon David Meara, Vicar of St Bride's, Fleet Street.

---

246 *Reflections in Middle Years,* published in 2005.
247 Thomas Pendry, Baron Pendry PC (born 1934), a Labour politician and member of the House of Lords.
248 Frederick William Augustus Hervey, 8th Marquess of Bristol (born 1979).
249 See chapter 6.

She had become friends with Mark Birley,[250] and at her first private dinner with him she gained an instant honorary membership of that same Annabel's, the most famous nightclub in the world.

She put on an important exhibition of her landscapes and portraits at the Russian Orthodox Cathedral in Ennismore Gardens in 2007, which was well reviewed and received. However, she told me her real love had now become modernist painting and sculpture, which I would not understand!

It is in that cathedral that I mostly see her now – reflecting, thinking, seeking, and, no doubt, receiving further inspiration for her future work.

Whither next? Who knows?

---

250 Marcus Lecky Oswald Hornby Birley (1930–2007) was a British entrepreneur known for his investments in the hospitality industry, founder of *Annabel's* (1962).

Index of Names

Aldous, Hugh, 17
Alexy, His Holiness Patriarch, 160
Amerasinghe, Terence, 90, 113, 118, 128
Astor, The Hon Bridget, 30
Astor, Lord, 30
Astor, Viscountess, 30
Avebury, Lord, 145, 146, 147
Belokurova, Julia, 163
Benedictus, Metropolitan, 27, 161
Berwick, Lady, 9, 10
Birley, Mark, 170
Blois, Sir Charles, 75
Bowes-Lyon, Lady Patricia, 2, 22
Bredin, General, 59
Bristol, Frederick, 8th Marquess of, 169
Bristol, Victor, 6th Marquess of, 39, 60, 80
Bristol, Yvonne, Marchioness of, 45, 162
Bura, Paul, 3, 5, 6
Buxton, Sir Thomas Fowell, 33
Cann, Major Mark, 154
Caradon, Lord, 71
Carrington, Lord, 138
Castro, Fidel, 122, 123
Catherine II, Empress of Russia, 65
Ciortan, Luigi, 130
Cobbold, Lady Blanche, 110
Cornelius, Metropolitan, 101
Crwys-Williams, Air Vice Marshall, 152
Culbertson, Crispin, 163, 166, 167, 169
Daneshmand, Bahman, 139

Dannatt, Lady, 106
Davidson, Jim, 94, 100, 150
Dean, Sir Patrick, 114
Denaro, Major-General Arthur, 152, 153
Deterding, Shirley, 61
Eban, Abba, 70
Elizabeth, Grand Duchess, 26, 27
Elizabeth, H.M. The Queen, 35, 38, 101, 137
Elizabeth, The Queen Mother, 35, 36, 37, 122
Foyle, Christina, 62
Fry, Elizabeth, 33
Gaddafi, Col Muammar, 140, 141
Gaddafi, Saif, 93, 95, 140, 141
Galitzine, Prince George, 69
Galitzine, Marina, 140
Galitzine, Princess Valentine, (Mrs John Meade), 23, 66
Gilliat, Sir Martin, 37
Gilmour, Lord, 71
Gladstone, David, 120, 122, 135
Glubb, Sir John, (Glubb Pasha), 46, 81
Gosling, Sir Donald, 152
Grabbe, Archimandrite (later Bishop) Anthony, 23, 79
Grabbe, Bishop George, 26
Guinness, Hon Desmond, 74, 86
Guinness, Jonathan, Lord Moyne, 74, 86, 145
Gurney, Major Anthony, 32, 89, 114, 125, 126, 169
Gurney, Christopher, 36
Gurney, Joseph, 32, 34, 39
Gurney, Patricia, 34, 125
Gurney, Richard (Dick), 72
Gulbenkian, Paul, 163
Hahn, Kurt, 12
Halloran, Paul, 100
Hammami, Said, 70, 85
Hammond-Innes, Dorothy, 61, 62, 63, 64
Hammond-Innes, Ralph, 60, 82

Hillam, Eileen, 77
Howe, Lord, 108
Hunt, Sir Rex, 152
Hussein, King, 47, 52, 155, 156, 157
Hussein, Saddam, 144
Jayewardene, President, 89, 90, 114, 116, 118, 127, 134, 138, 140
Jenkins, 1
Jennings, Dr Stuart, xix
Jumean, Ayman, 160, 161
Jumean, Eyhab, 140, 160
Jumean, General Shafik, 95, 96, 155
Kapoor, Mangal, 133
Kent, HRH Prince Michael of, 168
Kent, HRH Princess Michael of, 168
Kiril, His Holiness Patriarch, 1, 31
Knox, Father Ronald, 111
Kokoschka, Oskar, 68, 69
Laar, Mart, 140, 141
Lawrence of Arabia, (T. E. Lawrence), 48, 52
Lindstedt, Gunnar, 75
Llewelyn, Sir Dai, 130
Luik, Hans, 142
Lunt, Major-General James, 52
Lynn, Dame Vera, 152
Macmillan, Harold, Earl of Stockton, 110
Macmillan, Lady Dorothy, 110
Mattsson, Peter, 76
Meade, John, 23
Meir, Golda, 70
Mendoza, Andres, 24
Metcalfe, Steve, 130
Mishka, the Bear, 68, 69
Mohammed, HRH Prince, 157, 158, 160, 161
Mosley, The Hon Lady Diana, 74
Mosley, Sir Oswald, 74
Mountbatten, Earl, 128

Neville, Derek, 2
Nidal, Abu, 73
Obolensky, Prince Sergei, 67, 154
Oswald, Lady Angela, 35
Pendry, Lord, 169
Philip, HRH Prince, Duke of Edinburgh, 101, 114, 119, 125
Pitchforth, Vivian, 18, 20, 21
Potemkin, Prince, 65
Powell, Lord, 139
Premadasa, President, 91, 114, 119, 120, 121, 122, 126
Protasova, Vera, 98, 141, 166
Pym, Lord, 124
Racki, Ted, 154
Rajavi, Maryam, 143
Rajavi, Massoud, 144, 149
Ramini, Jafar, 94, 132
Reddaway, John, 71, 72
Richardson, Sir Michael, 141
Rix, Lady, (nee Gray), 109
Rix, Lord, (Brian Rix), 88, 104
Rodzianko, Michael, 66
Rodzianko, General Paul, 66
Rodzianko, Paul, 67
Rodzianko, Sergei, 65, 83, 84
Roche, Sir David, 141
Rothermere, Viscountess, 129
Samadov, Abdujalil, 139, 140
Savile, Sir Jimmy, 153
Saxe-Coburg-Gotha, H.M. King Simeon, 39
Secombe, Sir Harry, 152, 153
Shelton, Sir William, 75, 144
Slater, Admiral Sir Jock, 152
Smeekie, 18, 19, 21, 22
Summer, 97, 162 (see also Watson Summer)
Tebbit, Sir Donald, 124
Te Kanawa, Kiri, 162, 165

Thatcher, Margaret, The Baroness, 59, 77, 93, 100, 121, 123, 124, 137, 146, 151, 152, 153
Thatcher, Sir Denis, 141, 142
Thompson, Dorothy, 20
Trevelyan, G.M., 11
Trevelyan, Sir Charles, 11
Trevelyan, Sir George, 9, 115
Varvara, Abbess, 102
Waidyaratne, General Cecil, 134
Walker, General Sir Walter, 54
Wales, HRH Prince Charles, The Prince of Wales, 1, 38, 123, 153, 154, 156
Watson, Summer, 97, 162
Weinberg, Sir Mark, 107
Wijeyeratne. Dr. Nissanka, 91, 123, 127
Williams, Alan Lee, 113
Winn, Connie, 16
Wynne-Parker, Fiona, 125, 133
Wynne-Parker, Jennifer (now Lubbock), xix
Wynne-Parker, Michael, 59, 120, 132
York, HRH Prince Andrew, The Duke of York, 97, 162, 163, 164
Yugoslavia, HRH Princess Katarina of, 87, 94, 99, 152
Yugoslavia, HRH Prince Tomislav of, 99, 101

Printed in Great Britain
by Amazon